BURNING
THE
BOAT

By Mark A. Davis

Printed in the United States of America.

BURNING THE BOAT

ISBN-13: 978-1-7358663-0-7

(Lady Knight Enterprises Publishing)

Cover design and artwork created by Mark A. Davis

To have Mr. Davis perform a speaking engagement,
contact his office at 678 250-3287
www.burningtheboatbook.com

All Scripture quotations are taken from the New King James
Translation Version of the Bible unless otherwise indicated.

DEDICATION

To my parents, James and Edna Davis, for the simple, yet powerful gift of life, through God's goodness. The two of you instilled in me, by example, the virtues of honest, hard work. Thank you!

CONTENTS

INTRODUCTION

The comfort zone is one of the greatest enemies of mankind. It looks different for every individual, but it serves the same purpose, which is to hinder progress. Living in your comfort zone is like being a professional diver who refuses to get off the boat. However, that is about to change starting today. Yes! It's time to burn the boat and dive into your passion and purpose, headfirst.

We live in a world that has conditioned us to fear everything; fear of the unknown, fear of not having enough, fear of not being enough and fear of standing out. This fear fuels our thoughts, perspectives, and decisions. It is what becomes the driving force of our lives, and subsequently, also keeps us stuck in our comfort zones.

Right now, you are embarking on a journey of self-discovery, bravery and ultimately choosing purpose over a paycheck. At the end of this journey, you will find the courage to burn the boat and give up what feels safe and secure for the unknown pursuit of passion. I can assure you that it will be worth it in the end. You see, God has placed something special in each one of us and it is up to us to recognize it and ultimately, decide whether that is the path we want to take or not. The path you choose to take will determine the rest of your life. It is okay to feel fear, but it's not okay to allow fear to dictate your life.

Nelson Mandela once said, *"The brave man is not he who does not feel afraid, but he who conquers that fear,"* and he was absolutely right. Fear is something that none of us can escape because it will always be present in our lives. However, it is something that we can conquer.

When looking through the history books, all the extraordinary people who did noteworthy things are people who chose to rise above their fears. This does not mean their challenges disappeared, but it proved that fear is not powerful enough to stop you from pursuing your passion.

Fear is only as powerful as you allow it to be. If you give it time, attention, and influence, it will consume more room than you have permitted it to. What's worse is that we sometimes allow our fears to become our comfort zone.

You are tailor-made to carry out your individual assignment here on earth. This assignment fits your personality, your character, your physical makeup, including your personal experiences. Everything that has happened to you has been designed to shape you to become what you were intended to be, by the creator—God.

Imagine dying without actually becoming who you were meant to be. That is an incredibly sad thought and unfortunately, that is the reality of so many people who have passed away. Think of all those who were meant to be world-changers but left the world without making an impact. It is humbling, but also terrifying, that you could someday leave the earth, only to realize that you never discovered who you are.

So, brace yourself; a new season of your life has arrived! Therefore, drastic changes may start to happen in you and around you, that could potentially alter the course of your life. It's all up to you to embrace these changes or reject them. And remember, life is not constant, it's full of twists and turns, highs and lows, good and bad, night and day, and they all present themselves in different seasons of life. They all serve a purpose. Pay attention! You may be on the brink of a new season of your life.

Climbing the ladder of success in corporate America can be a daunting journey. It requires a certain level of discipline and a special kind of persistent attitude to truly make it. I think I can confidently say, I possessed those qualities. I spent decades working hard at climbing the corporate ladder and eventually earned myself a managerial position with a six-figure income. This is a great achievement by American standards and I'm sure, even the world over. I thought that I had truly arrived at my land of milk and honey at that stage, but little did I know that God had something even better than that, in store for me. I had worked so hard to get to this position and I was determined to enjoy every moment of it, and I did. Every day I looked forward to getting to my office and giving it my all. I had a great team working under me and great leadership above me. It was inspirational indeed. However, there was a downside to this. Like any success story, there were unpleasant moments where my ethics were challenged, my relationships tested, and sometimes my ability to produce outstanding work, was threatened by wrong judgments. I wish I could say it was stress-free, but it was far from it.

You see, when you are in this space where you need to feel secure, strong, confident, and relieved, the truth is, you are exposed to backstabbers, chess-players, and shallow-minded people who actually stifle your creativity and ultimately your ability to produce at your maximum potential.

If you can relate to all of this, and are looking for a way out, I want you to know that there is hope. You may not want to quit because you are making good money and have good benefits but realize that there is so much more out there for you. The corporate world may be your comfort zone or your safety net, and you may be afraid of losing the economic safety that comes from being a part of that world, but you will not arrive at the extraordinary until you let go of your fears.

Faith is a difficult concept for many to grasp, but I ask you this, if you can feel fear, why then can you not have faith? If both faith and fear require you to believe in something you cannot see, then why in the world would you choose fear? This is your time to burn your boat and follow the path to your purpose.

"Faith and fear both demand you believe in something you cannot see. You choose!" —*Bob Proctor*

CHAPTER 1

YOU'VE BEEN PLAYING IT SAFE

Like the majority of the population, my life was a conventional one. I made all the right moves, took all the right steps, worked hard, and did it with a good attitude; I basically followed the "how to succeed in corporate America" playbook to a tee. I was never complacent during my career, I spent decades doing everything right to achieve success, so it was no surprise when I did!

Adding to that, I've always had a natural inclination to see more of what the world has to offer. I'm considered a "trailblazer". My leadership type is described as a "disruptor," which, of course is best characterized as having a higher-than-average appetite for risk and a higher-than-average attachment to one's own personal purpose. I am true to myself in following my purpose, wherever it leads me.

Don't get me wrong, I loved my job as a Field Operations Manager. As a matter of fact, my job was amazing! I rose up the ranks pretty quickly, I was making a six-figure salary with benefits, and I had a great work environment. Having such a great job allowed me to put my kids in pretty decent schools, buy the best cars, and live in a nice home.

In short, it ensured that I had peace of mind, because all my needs were met, plus I had extra to help those around me as well.

My life was pretty great and even though I had everything, there came a point in my life where I felt as though something was missing. This nagging feeling was distracting, but I shrugged it off and carried on with my life, because I truly had nothing to complain about; life does not get any better than that.

However, my moment of reckoning came in 2019, when I took a trip to Ghana, Africa. I had been put on my second high blood pressure medication the previous year. So, while everything around me was great, my health was not optimal.

What I found in Ghana is something I will never forget. I quickly noticed that there were very few, if any, cases of cancer, high blood pressure, and depression. I wondered what was different between their lives and my own? And the answer was simple: they trusted God every single day.

You need to understand that these people didn't have much. They literally lived from hand to mouth, in poverty, but they were the happiest and most content people I have ever met in my life. All they had was faith in God; faith that He would provide, and indeed He did.

Throughout my Christian walk, I believed I had faith and that it was strong, but seeing how they lived their lives really rattled my faith and made me realize that I had been playing it safe. Yes, I was happy with my job and the people I worked with, but there had been something stirring in my heart that I had been ignoring, and at that moment it was calling out to me.

I asked myself this question: Why are we as Americans, the richest nation on the planet, not accessing this same God? Why are we not demonstrating this kind of faith?

You see, the media and peer pressure have conditioned us to believe that we need a lot of things in order to live our best lives, and the majority of these things are luxuries and not necessities. We have been conditioned into believing these things are what will ensure we live a wholesome life. However, this mentality has resulted in high stress levels, depression, hypertension, anxiety, and so many other health issues.

We are so consumed with working ourselves to the bone, just so we can afford to purchase things that are supposed to make our lives comfortable and bring us joy. But the sad truth is that most of us don't get to enjoy the fruit of our labor, because all of our time is allotted in the work itself.

I thought I had arrived because of all my achievements, but the truth is, I wasn't doing what I felt purposed to do, and that is the reality for the majority of the human race. Comfort has always been our greatest enemy, because in it we find complacency and mediocrity. You may be the richest man on earth, but if you are not fulfilling your purpose then you, my friend, are not living your best life.

"The mystery of human existence lies not in just staying alive, but in finding something to live for." —*Fyodor Dostoyevsky*

Thomas Edison is a name that will forever be on people's lips. He was a man who inspired and continues to inspire, millions of people around the world. Mr. Edison was not only a visionary, but he was a man who understood his purpose and engraved it on his heart. As you've probably heard, he attempted to create the conventional light bulb over 10,000 times. But while others mocked him, ridiculed him, and regarded his attempts as failures, he famously remarked, "I have not failed. I've just found 10,000 ways that won't work."

An intelligent and innovative man like him could have played it safe, found a conventional career with a stable job and income, and died a happy man… but he may not have died a *fulfilled* man. Thomas Edison has improved millions of lives, even long after his death, and it is all because he followed his purpose and not convention.

You have to pull the trigger!

In my case, I struggled with the decision, because I could not imagine what life would be like without my six-figure salary. But one of the amazing things about God is, He has a way in which He both communicates and comforts us when we least expect it. That day came for me when I met a surgeon in an airport.

The surgeon shared with me that he recently quit his $600,000 per year job. To everyone else, he was living the "American dream," in which he was, financially and professionally, but that was not the case for every other area of his life. "Why did you quit?" I asked him. To me he was a successful man in the prime of his life; I couldn't fathom why someone with his level of education, achievements, and thriving bank balance, would possibly want to leave that, especially because he was living in New York City.

He looked at me thoughtfully, before answering with full conviction and stated that after performing surgeries from Monday through Friday every single week, he would go back to his apartment and sleep the entire weekend. He also added that he became a physician because both his parents were physicians and wanted him to become one, as well.

As we talked and sipped on our beers, I could see the weight being lifted off his shoulders. He looked peaceful, happy, and free. He didn't have it all figured out, but the level of his faith gave him the confidence to pull the trigger. This man could no longer sacrifice his peace and sanity, just to live the dream.

You might be in a similar situation where you are miserable, exhausted, stressed, anxious, or even depressed, but you feel trapped in your situation, because you've got bills to pay. At the end of the day, your bills will continue to come, without fail, and that alone is enough to scare you into sacrificing your joy and purpose, for the sake of a paycheck.

"But my God shall supply all your need according to his riches in glory by Christ Jesus." – Philippians 4:19

I, too was in that situation. Deep down inside, I knew that my passion and purpose was to freelance, become an author, travel the world, serve more through ministry, (The Holy Land of Israel and to Africa) to help increase my abilities and natural desire to help people. I was at a crossroads with a very important decision to make, and I chose to pursue my passions.

What will people say?

We, as a society have been trapped in an endless cycle of debt, all in the name of surviving, when the truth is that most of what we own, we don't need. There are so many examples in the bible where God provided for His people. He provided for the entire nation of Israel in the wilderness; He provided for the Prophet Elijah in the wilderness; Jesus fed the multitude with just five loaves of bread and two fish. With such powerful examples, how can we doubt that God can provide for us in what we think are impossible situations?

Is money the most important commodity on earth? Absolutely. But is it the most important commodity for living a life of purpose? Absolutely not. The choice will always be yours, but if you ask me, I'd say it's time to stop playing it safe, and start putting your purpose first.

Questions like, "How am I going to pay my hospital bills, mortgage, student loans, etc.?" often plague our minds, talk us out of our faith and into fear and doubt. Often times, this leads us to believe that we will lose our independence and become a burden to our family and friends. Undoubtedly, these are very valid questions. However, these also become stumbling blocks to our purpose because they shift our focus from the main thing. So, why should you abandon what you have under control and expose yourself to uncertainty?

Think of it this way, Peter (the apostle/disciple) was in the safety of the boat; it was something he could control. I'm sure the other disciples probably thought he was crazy when he got out of the boat and walked on water to Jesus. I will bet they thought he was crazy, for even asking Jesus such an outrageous request! Even to this day, it sounds crazy, until you realize that while everyone else was focused on their own opinions and doubt, Peter actually walked on water!

You see, people may not agree with or even understand your decisions, but if you lend your ear to their opinions and abort your mission, you'll end up missing what could have been a once in a lifetime opportunity or experience. Your dreams are not meant to be understood by everyone. Playing it safe will never get you where you need to be. There is no glory in that.

The people who have left a significant impact on the world are all people who took risks. Whether big or small, famous or not, many have achieved great things in following their dreams, and you can be one of those people too.

Some people think my decision to leave corporate America is crazy and many have tried to talk me out of it. So, I want you to understand, this was by no means an easy decision; it was never going to be. I had to choose between playing it safe and just staying in my high paying job or taking a leap of faith, and following my passion.

The road won't be easy, but I can assure you that it's worth it. I don't wake up with regrets or wondering "What if" and that is because I made the decision by myself, for myself. Now, I'm not saying you shouldn't seek counsel from others, because it is, in fact, important, but their opinions shouldn't be the reason you walk away from your dreams.

Just to give you a little perspective on what I had to give up, take a look at my merit increase letter I received from my employer last year; it displays my salary increase. This is not me bragging, but rather, I want you to understand, this wasn't a decision I took easily or lightly, and I hope it encourages you to step out as well.

MEMORANDUM

To: Mark Davis

From: Human Resources

Date: December 11, 2019

Subject: 2019 Performance Review Rating and Merit Award/Salary Increase

This is to notify you that you received an overall rating of **3.28** on your 2019 performance review.

In recognition of your performance this year as reflected in your performance review and on behalf of ████, we are pleased to offer you a **2%** increase to your base salary. Your new bi-weekly salary will be $4,850.30 or $126,107.90 on an annualized basis.

The effective date for this increase is November 25, 2019 and will be reflected in your December 13, 2019 paycheck.

All other terms of your current employment with ████ remain in effect.

Congratulations on your increase and keep up the good work.

Sincerely,

MSS

Comfort zone or complacency zone?

Have you ever met someone who said they don't have to change something, because they are already good at it? Actually, a common phrase people like to use is, "Don't fix it if it's not broken." Now, this may be true for some aspects of life, but it is not true for your comfort zone.

I once heard a story about a woman who refused to apply for a senior position in her company, because she was already comfortable in her position. However, one of her junior colleagues took a leap of faith and applied for the position and got it! The woman became bitter against her bosses, especially toward the promoted employee in particular, who became her boss.

This is an interesting story because so many of us approach life with a similar attitude. So many people are more concerned with keeping their position, that they refuse to aim for something better, in the fear that they will lose what they already have.

There is a popular game show that has been around for a couple of years called, *"Deal or No Deal."* In this show, the contestant has to choose numbered boxes at random and eliminate amounts of money, after which they are offered an amount of money to end the game. What's fascinating about this show isn't the amount of money these people win, but rather the attitude towards the game and their willingness to take risks.

If you look into the record of winners for this show, you will find that only a few people have gotten to the end of the game, and even fewer have won the grand prize. Why is that? The answer is quite simple; the ones who got to the end, took the risk and stepped out of their comfort zone. These people had needs too; they were just as desperate for money as their fellow contestants, but they chose to have faith and go all the way regardless of the outcome.

Now, this is not what most people want to hear, because technology has made everything convenient, in that you can know the outcome of something before you begin. Unfortunately, life does not work that way.

The year 2020 has been a difficult one in which the world has been shaken by the COVID-19 pandemic. This pandemic has changed normal life as we knew it and has rattled everyone, especially those who were stuck in their comfort zone. People have had to come up with creative ways to make money, because they lost their jobs. In other words, they were forcefully ejected from their comfort zones as well as, forced to look within themselves and extract their potential, in order to survive.

The pandemic has had devastating effects on life in general, but it has also allowed people to realize that they are more than just employees. It has forced people to face the very things they were running from, and find creative solutions to problems that they thought could only be fixed through conventional methods.

What is standing in the way of you going after your dreams? As a person who worked in corporate America for 22 years, I can tell you that the peace and rest I began to have when I decided to pursue my passions, is like no other. Corporate America is no longer in the driver's seat of my life; I am no longer a victim to daily stress, anxiety, and pressure.

You can make the decision to stop playing it safe today. The truth is, when we take steps of faith, God is right there to meet us at our point of need. Yes, money is very important, but you don't have to slave away to earn it. Life is more than a 9 to 5 job, but you have to be brave enough to make that important decision of stepping out.

"Now may He who supplies seed to the sower, and bread for food, supply and multiply the seed you have sown and increase the fruits of your righteousness." – 2 Corinthians 9:10 (NKJV)

I don't expect you to quit your job like I did, because the truth of the matter is, many who are employees are actually not fulfilling their life's purpose in that regard. However, you have to realize that there is much more out there for you. You might be content in corporate America, but know that there will be challenges and compromises you will have to make in your journey. If you know that you cannot do that, then you need to muster up the courage to step into what you are really meant to be doing.

The corporate world is a jungle where you either 'eat or be eaten'. You can probably relate to having to do things that go against what you believe or what you're comfortable with, otherwise you risk being replaced. It is a place where creativity is stifled, depression is prevalent, and strife is part of the atmosphere. But don't be fooled into believing that you have no other options, or that your career will end the moment you step away from it. God will open new doors and bring you better opportunities that you never thought were possible.

Do not be afraid to sow your seed of faith today because our Heavenly Father will step in and multiply what you have sown. Remember, He is the creator of the Heavens and the Earth; there is nothing that is impossible with Him. So, what you need to do is to present your request to Him in prayer, stand on His Word, and believe (faith) that He will provide for you in any situation because He can and He will.

Just know this, you only live once! You have one life to live, so make the best of it; follow the path that sets your soul on fire. If Monday's make you miserable, or you hate waking up in the early hours of the morning every day, or if you can't wait for the day to end as soon as you wake up, then you, my friend, have been playing it safe, and you need to step out on faith.

CHAPTER 2

YOU'VE SHRUNK YOURSELF TO MAKE THOSE AROUND YOU MORE COMFORTABLE

Coming up in the corporate world is indeed a daunting task. The fact of the matter is, there isn't a spot at the top for everybody. You have to quickly decide on whether or not you have the confidence and gumption to reach for one of those few positions. If you are in the corporate world, I bet you are either gunning for the top, with fierce determination, or you have decided to settle in your level of employment. If you are the latter, then you need to ask yourself, "Why have I taken myself out of the running?"

Throughout my years in the corporate world, I have met many people who wanted a raise or a promotion, but didn't have the guts to go for it. The most common excuse I heard was, "I don't want to step on any toes," in reference to their co-workers, who were eyeing the same position. But this begs the question: Why would you shrink yourself to make someone else more comfortable? Why do we find it so easy to put other people ahead of us? Also, why is this considered humility? You came into the world alone and you will die alone. So, why should you waste the precious time you have here on earth, bowing to the needs of people who wouldn't do the same for you?

There is a fine line between being selfless and being a pushover. This may sound harsh, but it is a truth that many need to hear, grasp, and change.

Looking at all the most influential and inspirational people in the world today, one of the most common traits they all have in common is, they aggressively pursued their dreams by inserting themselves in spaces where they were not well-received; spaces where people tried to change them, because they (other people) either felt uncomfortable, or felt threatened by the presence of these game changers.

Right off the bat, you think of Oprah Winfrey- the first African American woman to anchor a news program. This was in the 70's, so I'm sure you can imagine the backlash she must have received and what her work environment must have been like. Nevertheless, she never failed to reach for her dreams, even if it took her to places that made other people uncomfortable. As the late Kobe Bryant said, "You have to be comfortable with those around you being uncomfortable."

We also have people like Henry Ford who went from working as an engineer in a motor company, to starting his own motor company because he had a vision. He was a person who took risks and didn't back down, even in the face of failure. I can imagine how crazy people thought he was with his ideas, but his perseverance is what made him the legendary innovator we still talk about today.

"When everything seems to be going against you, remember that the airplane takes off against the wind, not with it." – *Henry Ford*

There are many more exceptional people that can be named, but the point here is, stop putting yourself on the bench, when you are supposed to be in the starting lineup. Stop looking down on yourself and your abilities. Stop dimming your light, because you think it will make other people more comfortable.

You were created for a purpose, but you won't find that purpose if you value the opinions and feelings, of others about you, over your own. So, what if Sally will feel offended by your presence? So, what if John feels you are encroaching on his territory? Anyone who was there before you had the same experiences as you, therefore, you cannot bow out to make them feel more comfortable and secure.

Imagine if Albert Einstein had conformed to society's idea of normal? Imagine if Thomas Jennings had looked down upon himself as a Black man, and hadn't invented dry-cleaning in 1821? Imagine if Walt Disney had given up when he was told that he lacked imagination. There are numerous people who were mocked and ridiculed by society because they were different and it made "normal" people feel uncomfortable, but these are the people who played a part in pushing us forward as a society.

Get up and shape up!

One of the greatest inspirational movies out there is *Coach Carter*, which is based on a true story. This is a movie that continues to be relevant to this day, because of the lessons that it depicts. If you haven't watched the movie, it is about a basketball coach who returns to the high school he once attended, to coach basketball. But that's not all! The psychological state he found the students/players in, was heart-breaking. These kids had accepted failure and mediocrity, as a norm. They had no confidence or ambition, because from their point of view, reaching for more would be fruitless and dould only result in more disappointment. In short, these kids had already given up on themselves. They had conformed to what society said they would be. So, when Coach Carter stepped in, he not only transformed them as a team, but as individuals as well.

Each time I watch this movie, I can think of at least one person who, just like the kids, has given up before they even try, because their expectations were low, or they were afraid to break free from the boundaries that society had created for them, however, that has to change. Listen, nothing in your life or career, will move, if you do not believe it. Yes, it's that simple! You can have all the credentials and tons of experience, but if you don't believe in yourself enough to at least try, then everything else is pointless.

I know people who've been employed, and others who have been promoted, yet they were not the most qualified candidate for the position. Why is that? Because everything in life can be learned, but no one can make you confident, if you don't believe in yourself. You have to get up out of your pit of disbelief and put yourself out there; Shape up! You know your skills and abilities, so if you are lacking in an area that is vital to your progression, then get up and work on that, until you get it right!

It's time you stopped living in the shadows of other people, because you didn't think you were capable. The only person who knows what you are truly capable of, is you. Motivational speakers and books can hype you up and make you feel like you are able to conquer the world, but if you don't actually step out and do something, then all of that "motivation" is wasted.

You only live once!

"I'm just too busy!"

"I don't have enough time."

"I think so, and so is better suited."

"My idea is not as great as the other person's."

Sound familiar? These are just a few of the most common excuses that the majority of us use when we are afraid to do something. If your heart is racing, or your palms are getting sweaty, or you feel like you are being watched, then you have fallen into the, "What will they say/think" trap.

If you are a fan of classical music, then you have certainly heard the name, Ludwig Van Beethoven. Actually, you've probably heard that name even if you aren't into classical music. To this day, numerous musicians sample Beethoven's work in their music, and some of his best work can be heard in movies and plays as well.

But, what a lot of people don't know about Beethoven is that he suffered from hearing loss in his 30s. It still amazes me that some of his best and most famous compositions, happened when he couldn't even hear the music properly.

Too many people have become victims of excuses. Too many people have allowed their circumstances to dictate the value of their lives and have remained in a state of victimhood because they cannot see beyond their circumstances.

Each and every one of us has one life to live; and the catch is that none of us know how long we will be alive here on earth. Therefore, every minute that we spend alive is precious and should be appreciated, because we can never get time back. Almost every human has said the words, "I wish I had done this," or "I wish I hadn't done that," at some point in their lives, and have had to live with the pain of regret.

"As they came from their mother's womb, so they shall go again, naked as they came; they shall take nothing for their toil, which they may carry away with their hands." – Ecclesiastes 5:15 (NRSV)

I enjoyed my time in corporate America and the people I worked with, but sometimes I do regret not following my passion sooner. The more you age the more difficult it becomes to do things that were easy to do in your youth. But, the great thing about life is, that it is never too late to do something. You don't have to conform to what society deems as acceptable. Live your life to the fullest, because once you're gone, you're gone. Remember, you only live once!

You can be a game changer!

There is a fact in life that is undeniable and will always stand true: change makes people uncomfortable. The reason so many people are stuck in unfulfilling careers or situations that make them miserable is because they are afraid of change.

Change is something that requires you to step into the unknown blindly. Doesn't that sound terrifying? Not only are you entering unknown territory, but you are doing it without sight. No matter how you look at it, change is uncomfortable and unpredictable, which is why most people end up remaining right where they are because they don't have the courage to take that risk.

It is no secret that taking the path of entrepreneurship is a risk, especially when you do your research and see the statistics of how many start-ups have failed. I have overheard numerous conversations where one or both parties had a brilliant idea but decided not to act on it.

One of the best things about using public transportation is that you get to hear people's dreams. I cannot begin to tell you how many times I wanted to walk up to someone and tell them to go for it, because they had an amazing idea that could potentially change the world; that is one of the reasons why I was inspired to write this book.

You see, if only you can recognize your true ability, you will realize just how much you have to offer and probably be saddened by the amount of time you have wasted selling yourself short.

When I was faced with the reality of quitting my job to pursue my passion, it was one of the most difficult decisions I've ever had to make. I didn't think that my passion was anything noteworthy, or great enough to leave a high paying job, until one day God brought to my memory, the images of the people I had met in different countries, through missionary work. I remembered how grateful they were to receive help, even if it did not meet all their needs. God showed me that what I had been doing, no matter how minuscule it seemed to me, had greatly changed the lives of the people who had received that help.

See, so many of us think that in order to be a game changer, we need to be famous. The truth is, as long as you are making someone else's life a little easier, you have changed the game, and that's where many entrepreneurs miss it.

There was a young man who came to me seeking advice on his business venture. I listened to everything he had to say and felt proud because he had a fire in him that was driving him to persist until he succeeded. This was all well and good, until I asked him when he had come up with that idea and how long he had been working on it. Well, it turned out he had done all the planning (a great job at that) however, he had not started... at all!

I looked at him as though he had just sprouted a second head! I could not imagine how someone with such a great idea would do everything he needed to launch it, except actually launching it. He then told me of his best friend, who also happened to be an entrepreneur and was in a similar field. This young man's main concern was that he would lose his friendship, if he became his business competitor.

Now, while his worries were indeed valid, upon doing my research of his friend's business, I found that the young man had a far superior idea and could, in fact, become a leader in the market; that's how brilliant it was! Sadly, he was more concerned about his friend's feelings than pursuing something that would have made him great.

I'm not saying you should completely disregard the feelings of those close to you. What I am saying is, there's enough room for everyone to make it. People who truly love you will want you to succeed. Many people say, "There's only room for one at the top," but I beg to differ. Samsung, Apple, and now Huawei have had a healthy, spirited competition for several years, and all three remain leading technology brands.

There are so many motor companies out there, all of which are thriving despite people saying it's a saturated market. For so many years, people thought the makeup brands that have been around the longest would dominate the markets forever, and then came an influx of people who shook the market with their products and proved that nothing is set in stone.

When all is said and done, the answer lies within you. You can either shrink back and not do what you really want to do, so as to not offend someone, or you can be bold enough to make moves, even if people don't like it. Always remember that not putting yourself first is an injustice in itself.

You Are The Head, Not The Tail.

When you study creation and you observe God's plan and how he executed it, it is blatantly evident that human beings were created to dominate. We were created to be leaders in all spheres of life. However, the majority of us have surrendered that power to someone else.

"The Lord will make you the head (leader) and not the tail (follower); and you will be above only, and you will not be beneath, if you listen and pay attention to the commandments of the Lord your God, which I am commanding you today, to observe them carefully." – Deuteronomy 28:13 (AMP)

From the very beginning, God showed us that He had created each one of us with something that will require us to lead in some capacity. There is at least one thing within you that you are meant to dominate in, for His glory. So, you have to take off the blinders, that someone else is better than you, and focus on what you have within you.

The world marveled in 2019 when the new Miss Universe was crowned, and it was a South African woman with kinky natural hair in a pixie cut. Despite the mockery she received for wearing her hair that way, Zozibini Tunzi forged ahead with fierce determination and inspired so many women to love themselves and their hair. One of the greatest lessons that any of us can learn from Zozibini, is to not stand back for anyone. She didn't give up on her dream, even though her appearance made some people uncomfortable. As a matter of fact, that in itself fueled the fire within her to work harder and to succeed. And today, so many people are stepping into spaces that they couldn't before, because she showed them that it is possible, if you just believe in yourself.

The physician I had met at the airport gave up a lucrative career, despite the obvious backlash he knew he'd receive and took responsibility for his life and happiness. Even though he didn't have it all figured out, he still chose to no longer bow to the pressure of those around him and to put himself first. I know that the vast majority of people working in corporate are doing jobs that weren't their first choice. Moreover, many have jobs that they don't even like, but have been pressured into keeping them, to please other people.

This all begins in college, right? A lot of people come from households in which the parents or guardians dictate the career paths of the children, either to carry on a family business or legacy, or because the parents want their children to have the highest income possible. This is why so many employees are miserable in their positions, because they feel as though they have to obey and follow the path that was chosen for them.

Just like the physician who came from a family of physicians and was kind of forced into that career. Too many people are living miserable lives in which they have no control, just so someone else can glory in their achievements.

But your life is your own, and the person you need to satisfy first is yourself. If you are happy and flourishing, that is what will flow out of you to other people. You cannot allow someone else to live vicariously through you, no matter how guilty they make you feel for your decisions, because you are the only one who has to deal with the consequences.

Also, understand that you cannot please everyone. There will always be at least one person who is against your progress, because it makes them feel uncomfortable, or because they feel you will steal the spotlight from them. But, your life is not theirs to dictate. Your life is your own, and only you will be held accountable for the decisions that you do or do not make.

So, it is time you stopped living in the shadows. It is time you stopped being a follower in your own life and take up your position as a leader. You will be surprised at the opportunities that will show up, when you begin to live life as your true, authentic self.

"The individual has always had to struggle to keep from being overwhelmed by the tribe. If you try it, you will be lonely often, and sometimes frightened. But no price is too high to pay for the privilege of owning yourself." – *Friedrich Nietzsche*

CHAPTER 3

YOUR DREAMS SHOULD EXCITE YOU AND SCARE THE HELL OUT OF YOU AT THE SAME TIME

Do you know that giddy feeling you get when you're about to go on vacation? The thought of all the things you will get to see and all the activities you will participate in makes your heart race in excitement. Well, that's how you should feel about your dreams.

Corporate America is great for financial stability. When you see your amazing credit score and how much access to the system it provides, as well as all the benefits your job provides, it can be difficult to walk away from it all.

When I was younger, I was trapped in the belief that a great job was the key to my happiness. I thought that a high-paying job and a fancy office, equaled success. I thought that I would be fulfilled once I achieved this, but I was very wrong.

I had a dream within me, but it provided no financial security, neither was success guaranteed. I knew there was one thing I would get from following my dreams, that I would never find elsewhere, and that is fulfillment. My dream scared the hell out of me, because it required me to step out of my comfort zone, without a safety net.

I knew that it would challenge me far beyond anything else in my life and that the outcome would not only affect me but my family as well.

See, a dream is not just something that will give you satisfaction, it should light a fire in your bones; it should make you want to face each day with fierce optimism and eagerness. Your dream should keep you awake at night brainstorming and planning. It should make you want to jump out of bed every morning.

"Life is to be enjoyed, not endured. So follow your dreams, embrace change, and live what you love."– *Aysel Gunmar*

The moment you get that feeling- that fire in your bones- everything else pales in comparison. I too, never imagined I would be someone who would give up a sure thing to pursue the unknown, but I could not ignore the unction in my heart to pursue the dream that was rising in my spirit.

There is nothing better than doing what you love and living in your purpose. Waking up each day, living the life you were created for and doing the very thing that brings you fulfilment, is a feeling that can never be replicated, duplicated, or simulated.

Revive your dormant potential.

There's so much untapped potential lying dormant in all of us. It's high time we begin to look deep within us and draw it out. You may have fallen into a comfortable routine, that you're too afraid to give up on, even though you feel that stirring in your heart, to follow your dreams.

The unfortunate truth is, too many of us have become victims to complacency, and we do not recognize the dormant potential, lying deep within our hearts. There are so many game-changers and world-shakers out there right now, who are trapped behind a desk, with insane working hours, and you might be one of those people.

Time is something that none of us can be certain we have enough of, which is why every second we spend on earth is precious. Every dream or idea you've ever had, will die with you, once you leave this earth. Your children cannot inherit your vision, neither can they carry it on the way you would have, because that vision within you is unique to you. Now is the right time to gain the courage to step up, step out, and step into who God has called you to be.

Most Americans in the corporate world are using a mere fraction of their gifts, talents, and other God-given abilities. To a larger extent, life in corporate America, can be so limiting and depriving when it comes to allowing one to reach his or her full potential because you have to fit into a system that has already been tried and tested.

Unfortunately, you don't really see it this way in the beginning because your focus is on building a sustainable career for yourself and making enough money to live the "American dream." I hope and pray that as you read this book, your eyes will be opened to all the dormant gifts you have inside of you, because the world needs them, the world needs you.

Did you know that some birds learn how to fly on their first attempt? I was dumbfounded the first time I learned this fact. I tried to compare it to a baby who was learning how to walk and it didn't make sense to me to get it right on the first try. But, the more I looked into it, I found that birds have a natural instinct to fly, just as many components in our bodies have a natural instinct to perform in a certain way.

The birds figure out how to fly, and that they *have* to fly, because they are no longer in the safety of their nest. Their intrinsic nature to fly is activated when they step out of their comfort zone.

The moment they are rid of their boundaries, they get to experience the beauty that the world has to offer.

Just like birds, your true abilities will be hidden as long as you stay in the nest, confined to one thing, waiting for a paycheck every month, when there is so much you can do and so much you can achieve, if only you muster up the courage to leave.

"It's scary," is an excuse I have heard far too often, but that is the point! If it doesn't scare you, it's not worth pursuing. The reason our dreams scare the hell out of us, is they force us to believe we are capable of more than we ever imagined, because we are. So if it doesn't get your heart racing or your palms sweaty, then you need to lie down and dream again.

Punch the accelerator!

One of the most frustrating situations anyone can be in, is being stuck behind a slow driver when you are running late. I'm sure you can relate to wishing you could teleport into their car and punch the accelerator for them, but what if I told you that you are the slow driver in the front, backing up traffic?

You may not realize it, but by not releasing your potential, you might be holding back many other people from releasing theirs. Our destinies are connected to other people, so you might just be the key that someone else is desperately waiting for.

Take a computer, for example, it has so many components that are manufactured by different companies and without one of the major components, the computer cannot function. You can have a RAM, but it is useless without a CPU, just like you have multiple people on a production line.

By not fulfilling your purpose, you are hindering someone else's purpose, because human beings fit together like a puzzle.

I have always been fascinated by entrepreneurs, because they are among the most courageous people on earth. They took charge of their lives and stepped on the gas, to achieve their dreams, even though the statistics were not in their favor.

Listen, there will always be a million reasons not to do something, be it the economy, your bills, your family, whatever the case may be, but you will never find out what you can achieve, unless you actually try.

If everyone was discouraged by the statistics, we would all be stuck in unhealthy and miserable situations, just to make ends meet. As a matter of fact, none of the convenient inventions we enjoy today would have been created. Someone, somewhere, chose to ignore the negative reports and statistics, to pursue their dreams, and they made it.

Don't expect the road to be easy, because it definitely won't be, but one thing you can count on is, it will all be worth it when you arrive at your destination. What's even better is that God will be with you on your journey, ordering your steps and granting you the wisdom to make the right decisions.

"Fear not, for I am with you; be not dismayed, for I am your God; I will strengthen you, I will help you, I will uphold you with my righteous right hand." – Isaiah 41:10 (ESV)

It is okay to feel afraid and it is okay to have doubts and maybe even feel discouraged, but it is not okay to allow those feelings to force you into stagnation and complacency.

Most people have the "I gotta do what I gotta do," attitude, because they don't have the courage to step on the gas and get out of that place of mediocrity.

This does not mean that people who hustle and work hard doing what they have to do to support their families, are mediocre. This is talking about people who know that there is something greater calling out to them from within and instead, they chose to do what is comfortable and secure.

I felt this call on my flight back to the United States from Ghana on June 28th 2019. That is a day I will never forget. I had never been unhappy with my job, but when I felt that fire within me that day, I knew that I had been unfulfilled the whole time. See, the majority of us confuse happiness with fulfillment and that causes us to camp where we are, and refuse to progress.

Just because you are progressing in your career, does not mean you are progressing in purpose; never forget that. There is no accolade that will ever be greater than your purpose. So, chasing fancy titles and awards will only get your recognition within your circle, but it will not bring you true fulfillment.

Fighting the storm.

The journey of purpose is not an easy one. You will encounter storms along the way that will threaten to derail you, because the best things in life don't come easy. There will be times in which you'd have to defend yourself, your craft, your dream, and your vision. There will be times when it feels like the world is against you, but that is the nature of a storm.

I was painfully aware of the consequences that came with giving up my hefty salary and incentives and I knew that my family would be affected as well, but I still decided to step out, because I had learned the power of faith; I had seen it with my own eyes and I believed that the same God who took care of all those people in Ghana daily, without fail, would take care of my family too.

My journey taught me that following my dreams would require a lot of sacrifices, and that terrified me. I had invested 22 years into what I thought was my dream job; it was all I knew, and I was comfortable and complacent, because I enjoyed it and it allowed me to give my family the life I believed they deserved, but the burning passion within me would not allow me to give up on my dream, once it was unearthed within me.

Did you realize that all the reasons I mentioned, benefited me in some way? It's true, I was focused on my family and myself, so when God called me out of that place of comfort, my first instinct was to say "No". I did not want to give up what I had worked over two decades for, but each time I thought I wouldn't do it, images of my mission trips would float into my mind and remind me of the goodness of God.

I was reminded that I did not have to weather the storm by myself, because God was with me every step of the way. He was slowly building up the courage and faith within me, to take on the assignment He had created me for, so all that was left for me to do, was to heed the call.

"The Lord is good, a stronghold in the day of trouble; he knows those who take refuge in him." – Nahum 1:7

It will always be difficult when you think you are in it alone, but God is right there with you, even when you don't think he is. Challenge yourself today, to take that leap of faith and begin to pursue that very thing that sets your soul on fire; the thing that makes your heart race and gives you a smile, that lights up your face! Life is for living, not for slaving away in an office, building someone else's dream.

Whether you work in an office or on a farm, you will have to face multiple storms over the course of your life, but what's important is how you position yourself when you face these trials. Will you stand from a place of faith and conviction? Or will you allow yourself to be carried away by the storm?

It should bless you, not stress you.

I firmly believe that a life of purpose is a fulfilled and happy life. This does not mean you will not encounter challenges, because that's just a part of life, but it means that the weight of your challenges will not supersede the glory of your blessing.

Yes, bills, student loans, and other forms of debt are a very real part of life, but don't be deceived into believing, the only way out is by being an employee in corporate America. Whether you spend your whole life working for a big corporation, or you decide to pursue your dreams, there will always be obstacles you have to overcome, but one thing is for sure, your purpose will bless you, not stress you.

In all my years working in corporate America, the times I felt the most blessed and the most fulfilled, was when I was traveling to different countries on mission trips. I experienced a feeling that I'd never felt sitting behind my desk, but more importantly, I encountered God in a different way that I will never forget.

The more I pursued my purpose, the more blessed I felt. It's a feeling that no amount of money can buy. I felt more connected to my creator than ever before, and I loved knowing that I was part of something greater than myself. Every title I had meant nothing compared to the title of being a vessel God would use, to touch the lives of His people.

What I want you to understand is that you should not leave corporate America in vain, because you will end up being very disappointed. But, you should take that step, if where you are right now does not bless your soul. If you spend the majority of your life in corporate feeling stressed, then it's time you did a little introspection.

Your purpose may be to become an entrepreneur, or to teach, or to volunteer, or anything really, but it will be something that feeds your soul. Every day that you get to wake up should be cherished. Your time on this earth should not only bless you, but those around you.

One of the saddest statements I've ever heard in my life was from a young lady at church. I was walking by as she animatedly told her friends about a boy she had a crush on, but then she made this statement, "I would rather be miserable in a mansion, than happy in a shack." Every time I remember this day my heart hurts for the young girl. She spoke with so much conviction that her friends, who all tried to reason with her, failed.

There are people in the world today who are living with this mentality. They would rather live a miserable life, as long as they can afford to buy a few luxuries, as opposed to living a life of joy and fulfillment. And to that point, why do people think that following your dreams means you will go broke? Where did this mentality come from? Some of the wealthiest people on the planet achieved their financial success, because they followed their dreams, so where did we get the false narrative that people who pursue their passion will live in poverty?

Listen, the purpose and passion God has placed in your heart, will release a blessing into your life, because God's will for our lives is for us to prosper. That very thing you are afraid of pursuing is the key to unlocking the greater blessings God has in store for your life.

Now, I know that this isn't for everyone; it will never be, because there are people whose dreams are to conquer the corporate world, and if that is you, then I applaud you for following your dreams. But if that isn't who you truly are, then it's time you searched deep within your heart and asked yourself if you can live the way you are living right now, for the rest of your life.

We only get one shot at life here on earth. There is no rewind or pause button. Whether you like it or not, time will not stop until you make a decision. If great people like Colonel Sanders can achieve their dreams when they are old and grey, then it is not too late for you.

You can start dancing at the age of 30, and you can go to culinary school at the age of 40. Nothing has the power to stand in the way of you reaching your goals, unless you allow it to. If you arrive at a roadblock, just turn around and find another way, but the most important thing is for you to never stop moving forward, regardless of your circumstance.

Fulfilling your purpose is the pinnacle of success. Don't allow your life to become like an airplane that never leaves the runway, when you were born to soar above the clouds, like an eagle.

CHAPTER 4

YOU OWE IT TO YOURSELF

We are all aware of the narrative that putting yourself first translates to selfishness. This is amplified if you are a Christian, because you are told that putting the needs of others before your own is the right thing to do, and in many regards that may be correct. However, this is not true in all aspects of life.

As Americans, we are incredibly blessed to be citizens of this great nation. We have the freedom, opportunities, and resources to be whatever we want to be in life. We are blessed with the ability to create new careers and markets, which are something the majority of the world cannot do; that is why we are considered as a leader among nations.

Sadly, so many of us have been so focused on achieving the "American dream" that we have lost sight of *our* dreams. We have put ourselves on the bench to achieve what is considered as success. But let me ask you this, if you happened to die today, would you leave with no regrets?

Authenticity.

Authenticity is what everyone is chasing but very few are finding. When you watch or listen to any kind of interview, one of the most common words you will hear, is the word "authentic" and yet, you find that most of the people who use this word to define themselves look, sound, and act like someone else.

It is baffling and incredibly sad, that the one thing most people claim to be, is the very thing they are not. Are you authentic? Think about this; and if your answer is "yes" then what makes you authentic?

There is a popular saying in the Christian community that is so loved, that pastors and even singers, have used it over and over again, in songs, interviews, and even books, and that saying is, "to be broken."

Now, when most people first hear this, they fail to understand how brokenness is the key to finding yourself. See, being broken in this sense, is not a negative thing. It refers to getting to a place of complete surrender. Being broken, in this case, means you have done everything in your power and now realize that it just isn't enough. It is when you realize that true fulfilment will not come from what you are doing, because it is not in line with the authenticity of your purpose.

We live in an age where almost everyone wants to be a social media influencer. When you really dissect the life of an influencer, you find that very few are authentic. The majority promote the companies or brands that will bring them the most money, not the ones they actually believe in. An example of this is detoxing teas, that so many influencers have endorsed. Most of these people work out and eat right, or they use Photoshop to portray the perfect bodies, and yet they promote such products that could potentially be harmful to one's health, if used solely for the purpose of losing weight. What's worse is. a number of stories came out about a lot of influencers who don't actually use the products they endorse. That is definitely not authentic. So you see, the evidence is all around us, not just with social media influencers, but with many other aspects of life.

People are slowly losing their authenticity and thus becoming prisoners to a system, instead of having freedom in their purpose. Listen, anyone can imitate or impersonate someone else, but nothing will ever beat the original. For example, you can imitate your favorite singer all the days of your life, but the fact remains, you will never be that person no matter how hard you try. The only person you will ever be is yourself. So, why waste your life trying to be and do, what you are not? If you know deep in your heart that your passion in life is not sitting behind a desk and a screen, typing away all day long and attending long, drawn out meetings, or having to fight to keep your position etc., then you are not being authentic to yourself and it may be time to change things up. Do your best to find out what lights the fire in your bones, and work hard to attain it. Life is too short to not put your passion first.

It is honorable and responsible, to sacrifice your needs for the sake of your family, but you have to put an expiration date on that sacrifice, because it could possibly hurt you in the long run.

In all my years in the corporate world, I've seen a number of people having mental breakdowns, and others being rushed to the ER, because their bodies had slowly been breaking down. Corporate America is not completely negative, but it definitely isn't child's play. It is a place where only the physically and mentally fit survive.

It is a cutthroat environment that can chew you up and spit you out, if you are not ready. It is an environment that does not care about your authenticity, but rather the results you are capable of producing and whether or not they are beneficial to your company.

This is the reason why so many people don't survive in corporate America; they come in being authentic and soon realize that they will be required to make certain decisions that don't align with who they are. So, instead of losing yourself in a world where your time is limited, why not walk your own paths, where the essence of who you are can be appreciated?

"Your time is limited, so don't waste it living someone else's life. Don't be trapped by dogma – which is living with the results of other people's thinking. Don't let the noise of other's opinions drown out your own inner voice. And most importantly, have the courage to follow your heart and intuition. They somehow already know what you truly want to become. Everything else is secondary." – _Steve Jobs_

Talk to yourself.

Naturally, when people hear the words "Talk to yourself" they immediately think this will make them look crazy, but that's not quite what it implies. It is important to talk to yourself in a way that is uplifting. Words are very powerful and what we say determines what we believe, which ends up shaping our reality. What you say to and of yourself is what will manifest, because you are backing it up with faith.

The power of faith does not only apply to positive situations, it applies to negative ones as well. When you believe (faith) something, whether good or bad, you subconsciously begin to align yourself with that thought, thus causing it to manifest.

When you constantly speak words of life and hope over yourself, you don't realize it, but you slowly begin to act those words out, until they come to fruition. We have multiple examples of people who are/were brilliant with words and it worked to their favor.

One of those people was Muhammad Ali.

The heavy weight boxing legend was famous for mentally defeating his opponents with his words. Anyone who knows how any fight, war, or competition works, you will know, once you are defeated mentally, you are guaranteed to lose. Muhammad Ali not only knew how to use words to break down his opponents, but he also knew how to use them to uplift himself. He didn't wait for people to tell him what he was capable of, he said the words that he needed to hear *himself.* By removing that reliance on other people to validate him, he realized his true potential and it motivated him to work even harder to become the best.

People can only speak from the capacity of their mental or spiritual reserve, and the truth is, what they have to offer (say) may not always be enough to feed your vision. Another problem is, other people will not be able to speak what they don't understand.

For example, airplanes were something inconceivable in the minds of many, over a hundred years ago. I'm sure people thought it was impossible, until it was done. Because the majority could not understand it, they probably didn't have the right words to support this vision, until it was finally achieved by the Wright brothers.

Now think about this, how many people didn't believe it was possible? And how many people cannot live without it today? I can't say with certainty, that all the naysayers got to experience the wonder of flight, but I can say that it is so common today, most people don't stop to appreciate how airplanes have changed our lives.

The point is, if you want to get something done, talk yourself into it. Talk yourself into it until you believe, without a shadow of a doubt, that you can achieve it. You don't have to rely on other people to believe in you, because whether they do or they don't, you will only know what you can achieve if you believe in yourself.

Have you ever met a parent who tells their child they are so good at something when their child really isn't? For some children, that builds up the confidence they need to actually become good at the said activity, but for most children, it gives a false sense of ability, causing great devastation, when the public does not receive them well. I've heard parents tell their children that they are the most talented singer, when the child cannot even stay on key, and unfortunately, this gives the child a false sense of ability.

Why did I bring this up? Because not all support is actually good for you. Some people will support you, but subconsciously impose their goals or dreams on you. It's like the parent telling a child who can't sing that they can sing, just because the parent dreamed of becoming a singer when they were younger. The support may not be from a negative place, but it can have negative effects on you and what you want to achieve.

Listen, you were born into this world alone. No one else, besides God, knows the treasure that is buried within your heart, and no one can bring that treasure out unless you sign off on it.

This means, no one can bring out the authenticity of your gift if you don't believe in it. Just like no one, not even this book, will make you follow your dreams, until you believe in yourself. You will always have yourself; that is a fact. Everyone can forsake you, but you cannot forsake yourself. So, you owe it to yourself to live life in the way that will bring you the most peace. You owe it to yourself to wake up every day excited about what you have in store for the day. You deserve to have time to rest and enjoy life with your loved ones. You deserve to follow your heart wherever it will take you. The choice is yours. Don't be like me and many others who only got a wake-up call when their health deteriorated. As much as I loved my job, being put on a second high blood pressure medication opened my eyes and I quickly realized, that wasn't what I had envisioned my life to look like. I had to talk myself into leaving a sure-thing and following my passion, which I knew would also lead to peace and joy in my heart. My friend, no one can do it for you. You have to make the decision and be intentional about saying the right words to yourself, to keep your dream alive.

Stop being a tenant in your own life!

When you rent out a place, or become a roommate to someone who initially rented out the apartment or house, it is emphasized, one of the most important aspects to living there peacefully, is that you abide by the rules. You will find that you are limited to doing certain things, because you are merely a tenant; you have no say in the decisions made, by the owner or building manager. Most importantly, if you break certain rules, which are stipulated in contracts, the owner has the legal right to demand reparation or in extreme cases, can terminate the agreement. While this may sound unfair to the tenant, to the owner it is a perk. This is how life works.

When you speak to most people in the corporate world and ask them how they ended up in their careers, you will hear answers such as, "It's a family thing," or, "It was my mom/dad's dream," and other reasons that mostly have to do with other people. Yes, there are a number of people who are there because that career is their dream, but that isn't the case for the majority.

Being a tenant in your own life means, you have transferred the decision-making authority to someone or something else. You might think this isn't you, because a family member did not persuade you to go into that field, but if you went into it, for example, strictly because of the money, then you transferred that authority over your life to money, because it is what governs your actions.

Most people will read this and think I am saying, having or wanting to have a lot of money is bad, but that is not the case. As a matter of fact, having money is a good thing, because it gives you access to almost everything. But, what I am saying is, if your decisions are solely based on how many zeros are behind a figure, then you have a bit of a problem on your hands.

Money makes your life easier, but it certainly does not make your life happier, because it becomes like a drug; you can never have enough of it. Once you have some, you will want more and more, thus beginning a race that does not have a finish line. This pursuit will make you miss out on the things that really matter in life.

I was on a plane for one of my numerous business trips and overheard a conversation that broke my heart. These two men sitting behind me struck up a conversation about sports, that soon transitioned into the topic of family. One of the men was excitedly telling the other about how he got to witness his daughter's first steps and how grateful he was to have been there for that magical moment.

What surprised me was the other man's silence. He let out an audible sigh, which immediately had my attention and then went on to tell the other how he had missed all his children's firsts and further explained how he envied the close bond his children had with their mother. "They go to their mom for everything," he told his friend, "I know I work all the time, but I wish they would come to me sometimes." As the conversation went on, I learned that the second man worked an 80-hour week and barely got to spend time with his wife and children. He explained that he had to miss out on birthdays and important holidays, because his job was very demanding, but he continued working anyway, because he could afford to give his family the best that life had to offer.

What struck me about this conversation was, I could see myself in both their situations. When I began to work in the corporate world, everything else had to come second, because it was so demanding. I loved my job, but I hated missing out on important life events, because of my work responsibilities.

My job had taken ownership of my life and everything else, including myself, came second to it. I realized later on in life, I had missed out on doing a lot of things while I was younger, because all my focus and energy, was on climbing the corporate ladder, as that was where I had placed happiness, wealth, and good opportunities.

Most people have been living this way; as tenants in their own lives. Just like the physician I met at the airport, they allow other people to yield the decision-making authority over their lives, which often ends in disappointment. In the Physician's case, he had gone through pre-med, med school, and then specialized, which in total took him over a decade to obtain his qualifications, only because that was what was required of him. Think about it. This man wasted over a decade of his life doing something that pleased someone else. He became a tenant in his own life.

"You are blessed when you stay on course, walking steadily on the road revealed by God. You are blessed when you follow His directions, doing your best to find Him. That's right–you don't go off on your own; you walk straight along the road He set." – **Psalms 119:1-3 (MSG)**

Allowing other people or things, to dictate your choices is like walking off a clear path (the path God set for you) and trying to make your own path, in the thick of the woods. Neither will be easy, but the one that God set for you will always lead to joy, peace, and fulfilment. You owe it to yourself to live a fulfilled life; a life that you can be proud of. You owe it to yourself to live a full life with no regrets. Remember, there are no do-overs in life. You have this one shot to live out your dreams and achieve everything you've ever wanted.

If you chose to put yourself in the driver's seat, you will soon realize that it is worth pursuing your God-given passion, because that is where true satisfaction lies. Trust me, you don't want to live as a tenant in your own life, forever. Take back control and take back ownership of your own life. Yes, there is a lot of responsibility that comes with it and it will stretch you far beyond your comfort zone. In other words, it is a high price to pay, but it is a price that is well worth your freedom.

CHAPTER 5

YOU OWE IT TO GOD

The book of Genesis is one of the most profound books in the Bible. In it, we see the marvelous hand and heart of our Creator, as He created all living things. I've always found it interesting that the creation of mankind is mentioned in the very first chapter and that God made a clear distinction between us and the rest of creation.

"Then God said, 'Let Us make man in Our image, according to Our likeness; let them have dominion over the fish of the sea, over the birds of the air, and over the cattle, over all the earth and over every creeping thing that creeps on the earth.'" – Genesis 1:26

In the 26th verse of the first chapter of Genesis, we see that God made mankind in His image. To this day, a lot of people are confused by this passage of scripture, because they don't understand what the Bible means by the use of the word "Image." Human beings are a configuration of the attributes of God. He gave us dominion, free will, self-consciousness, and the ability to reason.

None of us were placed on this earth to merely occupy space; there is something greater that each one of us is meant to achieve. God has deposited something special in all of us, that we refer to as gifts or talents, which ultimately leads us to fulfill our purpose here on earth.

Have a servant attitude!

We are all servants of God, called to different functions here on earth. Each one of us -whether strong or weak, young or old, disabled or fully abled- have been blessed with some sort of gift or talent. No gift is superior to another. We are like pieces of a puzzle; each piece is unique, but they all serve a common goal.

With this knowledge, realize and accept, you have something to offer. The mistake the majority of us make is, comparing what we have to what others have. A company employs people with an array of specialties that are vital in their individual roles, but each one of them brings something valuable to the company as a whole, more especially if they have the attitude of being there to serve.

"Service to others is the rent we pay for our room here on earth" – *Muhammad Ali*

Your gift is not meant to serve you alone. I have met countless people who spend their days worrying about and working, solely for themselves. These people are one-track minded and believe that their lives are all about providing for themselves and their families, but that was not God's intention.

When God created us, He intended for us to be creatures of community. Jeff Bezos created Amazon, Anita Roddick created The Body Shop and Ingvar Kamprad created IKEA. These and many more people, stepped into new avenues that met a need in society.

All of us have the intrinsic ability to recognize needs, but very few of us will actually step up to the plate and do something about it. That is because we live in an inherently selfish society. But when you observe these wildly successful entrepreneurs, you find that their main objective was to serve society in some way.

Serving others is the best way to discover yourself. When you genuinely do something to help someone, that action unlocks hidden gems within you. Successful entrepreneurship is not about making bucket loads of money and being your own boss, it is about finding a need, and meeting it in a sustainable way.

A philanthropist will give a hungry man a fish, which is quite noble. An entrepreneur, on the other hand, will employ the man, teach him how to fish, and expand his fishing business. Already you can see that the entrepreneur has empowered the man by teaching him a skill and giving him a job that will bring him continuous income.

It is a high honor to serve others; that is a common purpose among us all. God has gifted you with something that will change the life of at least one person. Hiding away and being passive serves no one but yourself, which only results in a life of regret and unfulfillment.

Seedtime and harvest.

The principle of seedtime and harvest applies in all forms of gifting. As long as the earth remains, there will always be a time to plant seeds (work) and a time to harvest the fruit (enjoy).

The problem with slaving away in corporate America is that you find yourself stuck in the planting season for far too long. You can receive several promotions, but as long as you are not releasing the gifts God gave you, you are stuck in the planting season.

I witnessed this numerous times working in the corporate world. People would come in fresh and excited to work and slowly but surely, I would see their light dim. Their initial passion would fade away, because they spent so much time working that they had no time for anything else in life.

They would work so hard, but not get to enjoy what they were working for.

Your gift is a seed God has deposited in you. It is your duty to plant your seed in the right soil, in order to enjoy its full benefits. Your gift is what opens new doors of opportunity and allows you to serve your Creator and the people around you. You can make a difference in the space that you have been placed in.

Focus on what has been given to you.

One of my favorite stories in the Bible is that of the three servants and the talents, found in Matthew 25. This also happens to be one of the most famous stories in the bible and thousands of sermons have been written based on it. But, while everyone focuses on the third servant, I was more interested in the first two. Just for the sake of context, I did a bit of research and found that a talent is equivalent to almost $1.5 million today.

With this in mind, it is obvious that the third servant was actually entrusted with a substantial amount of money... and he did nothing with it. Now, the reason why I find the first two servants more interesting than the third, is because they immediately sprang into action, without fear or hesitation. They took what was given (gifts) to them and didn't hold back with releasing it into the world. Thus, it produced a great return that the master was proud of. Because these two servants proved to the master that they were trustworthy, wise, responsible, and ambitious, the master blessed them with more. Don't be like the third servant who went and buried his gift, because there is no glory or blessing in that.

I find this interesting, because it always reminds me that God expects me to step out in faith and use what He has given me, for His glory.

In the story, the third man buried the talent that was given to him, and sadly, that is the reality for the majority of people in corporate America.

So many people are dying on the inside, working a job that they don't even like, feeling exhausted all the time, and constantly being under extreme pressure, just so they can get that paycheck at the end of the month, that they don't even get to fully enjoy because they have very little to no free time.

God didn't create us to be slaves to a system, He created us to be servants who give back into our society, by using the gifts He gave each one of us. If you know that you are destined to be and do something, other than what you are doing right now, then you need to make some serious life decisions.

I once read a thread online about people who had given up great jobs to follow their passion, but there was one in particular that stood out to me. The young woman stated that she worked 9-5 every week. Her job always left her exhausted and uninterested in pursuing anything other than her work. She went on to say that she knew in her heart, a job in corporate was not for her. Her passion was in helping other people and traveling the world. So what did she do? She quit her job and decided to become a flight attendant, which was a career in which she would get the best of both worlds.

God did not make a mistake with you. I hear people say too often that God made a mistake in giving them a gift that was too much of a burden for them. But you see, God will never give you something that He knows you can't handle. Unlike the systems of the world, God is not trying to trap you; that very passion you have within is the key to your true success. But like everything worth having, it will not come easy.

So you see, following your purpose is not about becoming an entrepreneur. It is solely about finding the passion that is alive inside you and expressing it in a way that aligns with your God-intended purpose.

"For we are his workmanship, created in Christ Jesus for good works, which God prepared beforehand, that we should walk in them." **– Ephesians 2:10 (ESV)**

The problem that the majority of us make is, we tend to limit ourselves before we even give it a shot. But, we owe it to our creator to be the best version of ourselves that we can be. Anyone who has ever invented something, never stopped until they had perfected it. Today, all these products and technologies we love so much, are the perfected versions.

Understand, you were created because the gift within you was already perfected, but it needs to be discovered and uncovered. You have the right and the freedom to be exactly who God created you to be, but you have to have the courage to let go of your safety net, otherwise you will never break out of the chains of mediocrity.

The nature of God-given gifts.

There are natural and spiritual gifts, and all come from God. What we call natural gifts and talents, are those you are born with. They are discovered as you grow older through interests and inclinations. We normally say that one is naturally talented when that is the thing predominantly seen in that person's life.

One of the most obvious gifts in my life is that of writing. I love to write about everything; what I'm thinking, what I've seen, what I plan to do, etc., but I always viewed this as a hobby and never as a gift. It was only when I came to the realization that I had to leave the corporate world, did I begin to recognize this gift and what it could potentially evolve into.

From a different point of view, look at your life as a gift from God to humanity. You are meant to be invested in the soil of human life and just like a seed brings forth more of its kind (reproduces itself), so are we as humans, supposed to multiply ourselves. You are an investment that should be profitable to someone else.

Many people think servanthood can be equated to slavery, but that is the furthest thing from the truth. Think of it this way, when you help an old man or woman cross the street, it does not change your nature as a person, or take away your identity; it does not mean you have to then do everything else for the old woman as well. Being a servant in God's eyes is doing what is right and good at all times, especially when it's not beneficial to you. Your gifts are in you, but they were not intended for you alone. Think of music and how wonderfully diverse it is. The millions of artists around the world are all gifted in the art of making music, but their gift only reaches a particular audience. Yes, all the musicians create music, but their music is appreciated differently by different people. Do you see how wonderfully complex your gift is now?

What about the people who give up their jobs to start an orphanage? These are people who have the gift of compassion, and while their job might not be glamorous, they are actively assisting children/people who have been abandoned, to find their place in the world, thus guiding them in the right direction, to fulfill their purposes.

We were created to fit together like a puzzle. Every last one of us has a part to play to contribute to the bigger picture.

God empowered you to do and achieve certain things; wouldn't it be a shame to let it all go to waste?

God loved us so much that he created us to be unique, and to bear fruit for the good of all humanity. We owe it to our creator to reach our full potential and release all the gifts He so generously deposited within us. Just think about this, your minute of obedience could be the breakthrough someone has been waiting on their whole lives.

"When I stand before God at the end of my life, I would hope that I would not have a single bit of talent left, and could say, 'I used everything you gave me'." – *Erma Bombeck*

CHAPTER 6

YOU OWE IT TO YOUR FAMILY

Each one of our lives is part of a community in some shape or form, and the truth is, what we do and what we feel, affects those around us the most. Being able to protect and provide for our families is not only a priority, but for a lot of us, they are our primary motivation for working as hard as we do and because of this, it is difficult to walk away from a stable source of income.

When I made the difficult decision of walking away from my great job, in the corporate world, my mind was immediately flooded with negative thoughts such as, "Will I still be able to take care of my family?" and "What happens if I fail?" and before I knew it I had discouraged myself, and this is something that I've witnessed many others do as well. While you might think it is selfish to quit your job and follow your passion, it is more tragic to spend your life building someone else's passion. It is definitely not wrong or shameful to experience doubt and fear, but allowing them to hinder you from discovering your full potential, is a big problem.

Picture this: You are 85 years old, well into retirement, but instead of enjoying the rest you deserve, you spend your days trying to find something to do that will make you feel fulfilled. One day, out of the blue, you receive a video and this video shows you everything you were capable of achieving and what your present-day would have looked like, had you followed that route. How would you feel?

Just like me, you may have entered the corporate world with a lot of energy and determination to succeed, and maybe you even reached the professional goals for yourself. In fact, you may even think, "Ah, this is not so bad," especially when payday rolls around, but when all is said and done, what is it that you really achieved?

I realized that my fear of disappointing my family could not only become a stumbling block to me, but also, it was not as bad as disappointing myself. Yes, I thought about all the bills I had to pay, the children I had to educate, and thought I had to be selfless for them, when in fact I was achieving the opposite. By not following my passion I was robbing them of a better life for generations to come.

When my doctor told me that he was putting me on a second blood pressure medication, I knew that I needed to make some major changes to my life. I loved my job, but I could not deny that it was very stressful and very demanding and it had taken a toll on my health. When I was confronted with how badly my health had deteriorated, I realized that I would not be able to provide for my family if I were dead, and I was not ready to go any time soon.

My point is, don't wait until it is too late to make that decision. Don't be like me and wake up one day feeling your body failing you. I will say this again, it is simply not worth it. You might think your family needs all the fancy things you are providing for them, but if you ask them, they will tell you they need you alive.

The effects that the corporate world has on mental, physical and emotional health are very real and can sometimes last a lifetime. So, don't ignore them just for all the zeroes you see at the end of your paycheck, because none of those zeroes can give you back your health, once you lose it.

I know that having money gives you access to the best medical care, but what I'm saying is that even the best medical care does not have the power to restore your health to 100%. So don't waste your life and your health on something that will only benefit your family, if you are alive.

You owe it to your generation and beyond.

When you're older and look back at how you've lived, do you think what you're doing right now will benefit the generations to come? Are you building a legacy for your children, grandchildren, and great-grandchildren?

Most of us had to endure the pain and suffering that comes with starting from the bottom, but the truth of the matter is that there are those whose paths were much simpler and stress-free, because they were heirs. Even the sorority system that we have in colleges, grants advantage to the children of its former members. So you see that there are certain systems that govern society, and you can be the one who paves the way for your family and future generations. The cold, hard truth is, your children cannot inherit your degrees. You can work as many hours as you want (building someone else's legacy), but that position you currently hold will not be passed down to your child. So in essence, you are wasting away all your strength-filled years helping someone else secure their family's future... but what about yours?

As I've mentioned, all the good inventions we enjoy today are products of people who were true to themselves and followed their dreams. It is those dreams that have left a lasting impact long after the owner passed. Because those people followed their dreams, their names will always be mentioned as though they were still here, because they live on through their creations.

For example, we're enjoying electricity today, because Benjamin Franklin believed it was possible and risked his life experimenting with a kite and lightning just to prove his theory. The many scientists who built on Benjamin Franklin's work are also to be credited for this life-changing discovery. But the point here is, Mr. Franklin created a foundation for the other scientists to build on, which is what we should be doing for the upcoming generations. We owe it to our families to create a platform for them to follow their dreams, unashamedly.

There are people you don't know who will be sustained, because you wrote that book, or took that trip or made that financial contribution or created that product. Never underestimate the power of your contribution to life. You may not think you have an impact on anyone, but you're wrong. There is always someone looking at you, wanting to be like you, wanting to learn from you, even if you don't realize it.

As small as worker ants are, with every particle of dirt they carry, they are able to build a huge anthill. Your contribution to life, as insignificant as it may appear to you, will go a long way in touching the lives of people you may never even get to meet.

You can outlive your life!

Your family can learn a great deal from you, but one of the most important lessons you can teach them is having the courage to follow your dreams. Most, if not all of us, have been inspired by someone at some point in life or we have someone that we look up to and wish to be like. This is because of the legacy they left behind or have created.

Take the Hilton Hotels, for example. Conrad Clinton, the founder of the Hilton Hotels, invested $5000, as well as his time, ideas, and creativity, into building his empire. Even now, 100 years later, the Hilton legacy lives on and has afforded his children, grandchildren, and great-grandchildren, a financially secure life.

Imagine doing something that will secure your family a hundred years from now? That is the kind of forward-thinking that builds legacies; it goes way beyond just providing for your family today. Your goal should be to empower your family to do what they love by doing what you love.

"Never continue in a job you don't enjoy. If you're happy in what you're doing, you'll like yourself, you'll have inner peace. And if you have that, along with physical health, you will have had more success than you could possibly have imagined." - *Johnny Carson*

Let's be real, leaving your cushy "safe" job takes some serious guts, especially when you have people depending on you, but that is even more reason for you to dive right in. I know it sounds crazy, but it is the only road that leads to greatness. Your comfort zone is not a place you are meant to dig your roots in.

I know all about playing it safe and weighing out the pros and cons, because I did that. But, it only led to giving myself reasons as to why I shouldn't pursue my dreams. What I'm trying to say is, you should think and plan, but don't think too long and don't think too hard. Overthinking things will only lead to discouragement, frustration, and maybe even depression. The longer you spend trying to figure everything out, the faster you talk yourself out of it.

One of the biggest mistakes you could ever make is thinking that your family only relies on you for financial support. Working in corporate meant spending less time with my children, missing games or recitals sometimes, as well as important milestones, but when I made the decision to leave the corporate world and become an entrepreneur, I realized that I didn't have to sacrifice time with my family just to provide.

The rich young ruler.

There's an interesting story in the 19th chapter of Matthew about a rich young ruler who asked Jesus what he should do to obtain eternal life and Jesus told him to sell all he had and follow him (Jesus), the young man walked away with a sorrowful heart.

"Jesus said to him, "If you want to be perfect, go, sell what you have and give to the poor, and you will have treasure in heaven; and come, follow Me. But when the young man heard that saying, he went away sorrowful, for he had great possessions." – **Matthew 19:21-22**

I liken the decision the rich young ruler had to make to the one you have to make, between staying or leaving corporate America. Although the circumstances are vastly different, the idea is to highlight the difficulties in both.

I can only imagine what was going through the rich young ruler's mind when Jesus told him to give up everything he had. He might have had thoughts like, "What will my family say?" or "People will laugh at me," or "It's too much to give up," and you might be in the same boat, wrestling with similar thoughts.

The truth is that it won't be easy. By stepping away from a job you've worked so hard to obtain, you are making a great sacrifice that will affect your family as well, but I'll tell you from experience, you owe it to yourself and your family, to be the best version of yourself.

The rich young ruler had no idea that following Jesus would have been the greatest decision he would have ever made in his life, just like entrepreneurs Shep and Ian Murray, (brothers) who gave up their fancy jobs in the corporate world, to sell ties out of their backpacks. These men chose their passion over their paychecks and "Started making neckties instead of wearing them," as one of the brothers- (Ian), puts it.

The Murray brothers are the owners and founders of the billion-dollar business, "Vineyard Vines" and this is all because they dared to leave the corporate world, to do what made them feel fulfilled. Without a doubt, this decision they took was a risky one for themselves and their families, but in a quest to be their most authentic selves and to do what made them feel alive, they built something that has ensured that the generations after them, are well taken care of.

Now, maybe you're not a big dreamer like the Jeff Bezos' of this world, but know that whatever you choose to do, in whatever capacity, as long as it is authentic to you and in alignment with your purpose, it will provide for you and your family, as well as bring you peace and fulfillment like no other.

It's okay to create your own path.

There's something that every country has in common: family businesses. On my numerous trips to various countries, I found that some cultures and families don't allow their children to have their own dreams, or even get an education. The only choice that most of these children were given, was to work in the family business, when they got older.

Many of us may not come from families that own businesses, but maybe we come from households that dictated what we studied in college and the career paths we eventually took. Conceivably this is why there is so much dissatisfaction amongst people working in the corporate world, because they are busting their necks living out someone else's dream.

I once heard a parent say to a child, "I gave up my studies in nursing because I was pregnant with you, so you have to finish what I started." It was one of the most preposterous things I had ever heard, and when I met the physician at the airport, I got to see the result of forcing someone to do what they don't love.

All of this is to say that your family loves you and wants the best for you. A lot of us believe that our loved ones expect us to do certain things in order to garner their affection and acceptance, when the truth is, love is unconditional and the people who love you want the best for you too.

You will provide the best life for your family when you are fulfilled, because people respond to what you give and show them and you can only give out of the abundance of what you have inside you. Therefore, don't hold yourself back thinking it is the best decision for your family, because the best decision is the one that will enable you to be happy and healthy.

Don't be afraid to have honest conversations with your loved ones about your feelings. Remember, you only get one shot at life, and it is way too short to spend on anything else other than what sets your soul on fire.

Always remember that moments lost and memories missed can never be replaced or duplicated, just like you can never repeat any minute of yourself, because once time has passed it is gone forever. Don't miss out on those special moments with your family, because you have a deadline. Don't put your family second by working yourself to the bone, in an attempt to put them first because trust me, they would rather have you alive and well than any gadget money can buy.

CHAPTER 7

YOUR FAITH IS YOUR MOST PRECIOUS POSSESSION

Faith is one of the most important elements of life.

For most of my life, I thought the opposite of faith was fear, but as I got older, I realized that the opposite of faith isn't fear, but unbelief. Why? Because fear is also a product of faith. You see, faith is an unwavering belief in something, so if you are afraid of spiders, for example, then you have an unwavering belief that all spiders will harm you somehow. Most people are afraid to become entrepreneurs because they are afraid of failure, of what people will say, or losing their comfortable lifestyle, thus their faith works against them. On the other hand, faith is also what helps you discover your purpose in life. It propels you forward in your lowest moments, because it triumphs over doubt, anxiety, and fear. It is a powerful force that anchors our lives and without it, we are merely beings running blindly in a maze.

"Both faith and fear require you to believe in something in which you can't see, you choose." – *Bob Proctor*

Fear is a lie!

Do you remember the story of the spies that Moses had sent to find out what the land had to offer? Twelve spies went out and all saw the exact same things, which were the land was indeed flowing with milk and honey and that it was rich in mineral resources. They also saw that this land was inhabited by giants, and that was a game changer. All of them saw the same thing, but they didn't perceive it the same way.

Ten of the twelve spies concluded that it was impossible to possess the land because giants inhabited it. They had already accepted defeat before the battle was even a concept! Their fear made them forget that God was on their side; the same God who had delivered them from hundreds of years of slavery at the hand of the Egyptians; the same God who parted the sea that they walked through on dry ground.

But the other two, Joshua and Caleb, believed the word of the Lord. They stood firm in faith, believing that they could conquer the giants, because God was on their side. They saw the victory from the eyes of faith, which is why they got to see and dwell in the Promised Land, while the others did not.

See, what you believe is what will manifest. Fear is something that will always be around, but you have to choose if that's what you want to base your decisions on. If you allow fear to hold you back from breaking off the shackles of the corporate world, then you will have to bear the consequences such as misery, sickness, exhaustion, and sacrifice.

Fear is like a magnifying glass. It makes you feel insignificant and powerless. It brings the object so close to you that you can't tell exactly what its true size is. It creates the illusion that the thing you are afraid of is far greater than it actually is and that it has the ability to conquer you.

Therefore it is time you stopped focusing on what could go wrong and start believing that everything will go right. Believe in yourself and your abilities, but more importantly, believe in your creator and trust that He deposited in you all that you need to succeed.

If you succumb to fear it will cripple you and cause you to miss out on opportunities. It robs you from living life to the fullest. It's like flying on autopilot, you'll still be moving, but you won't experience the thrill of controlling the plane.

Joshua and Caleb refused to be influenced by the magnifying glass of fear like everyone else. They recognized the giants (obstacles) for what they were, but more importantly, they didn't lose sight of who God is. Their grip on the handle of the promised inheritance (from God), was so firm that they would not let anything, even giants, take what was rightfully theirs, as God had said. This didn't mean the giants would somehow disappear and it would be smooth sailing from then on. The giants were a reality, but their faith in God overcame their fear of the giants.

Their confidence was a product of their faith in God and His promises. He had told them that it was theirs to inhabit and they believed Him. This confidence is what you have to apply to your dreams and passions, you have to hold on to it, by all means necessary, because there will always be challenges to face, some bigger than others, but if you stand firm in your faith, God will part the seas for you; He will *always* make a way.

"Fear not, for I am with you; be not dismayed, for I am your God; I will strengthen you, I will help you, I will uphold you with my righteous right hand." – Isaiah 41:10

Prepare your heart for change.

How prepared are you for a new phase in your life? Let me clarify, is your heart ready for a new phase of life? This is an important question to ask yourself, and if your answer is "No" then you need to pause and make things right first, before you proceed.

Now, I know this isn't what you want to hear, especially if you are bursting at the seams with excitement, to finally live in your purpose.

The process of preparing your heart for new beginnings, varies from individual to individual, based on many factors. Maybe your heart has been broken over and over again, by people you trusted or maybe you feel anxious, unprepared and afraid, or maybe you don't feel mature enough, to carry the great responsibility as an entrepreneur, so don't rush.

Think of how much preparation farmers need to do before they plant the seeds. They need to prepare the soil and make sure it has the right kind of nutrients for their climate, as well as the type of seeds they will be planting, and with this information, they can also choose the right fertilizer, and so on.

Leaving the corporate world is like abandoning grocery stores and growing your own produce. The former may be more convenient, but it is also the least rewarding. Like a farmer, be patient with yourself and be intentional about building your character and strengthening your faith, so that you will be able to withstand the storms, (challenges) when they come.

I firmly believe that the majority of people encounter failure, because they did not plan adequately, and I'm not referring to finances or resources, I'm talking about building character. If you observe your current bosses, you will realize that they each have certain character traits that enable them to be effective in leadership, at whichever level or position they currently hold.

Act on your convictions.

What do you believe about yourself, and what lengths are you willing to go to, in order to transform what you believe into reality? Do you believe that you are well able to achieve whatever you set your mind to? Do you believe that you are smart, creative, and ambitious enough to start a business, run it, and turn it into a success? These all seem like simple questions, but you'll be surprised to find out just how much you doubt yourself, when you ask yourself these questions and allow honesty and vulnerability to lead you to the answers.

I thought I was very confident in my abilities, intelligence, and education, until I was faced with the decision of leaving my safety net (my job) and following my own path, as an entrepreneur. I thought I was secure within myself, until I realized that I would have no one to answer too and no one to tell me what to do.

Do you remember the first time your parent or guardian trusted you enough to leave you home alone? Although they gave you specific instructions and you felt you were old enough, the moment they walked out the door, the reality that you were alone sunk in and you had a brief or prolonged moment of panic, before you settled into a good rhythm and felt comfortable being alone.

Did you know that a brief moment of panic has the ability to make or break you and if you don't act on your convictions, you will find yourself stuck in an endless cycle of mediocrity, because you will convince yourself that your safety net is permanent. But the issue with safety nets is that when they wear out, they will give out, when you least expect it.

To break the cycle of doubt in your life, you've got to exercise faith. Get information, believe it, and then act upon it. You'll be surprised at how much you can achieve, just by acting upon what you believe. It's always encouraged to acquire skills, but the lack of skill should not be a reason to delay. Avoid acting based on what you see others doing; it may not work for you. Develop your own convictions and forge ahead boldly.

You need to have your own stand on issues that affect your wellbeing. What's your take on politics? What are your thoughts about the economy? Marriage and divorce? Crime and so forth. If you don't have an opinion, you will find yourself following the crowd, blindly. Let me conclude this thought with a true story that happened to a friend of mine.

He was on his way home one afternoon after visiting me. During the short walk back to his home from mine, he saw a group of people running in his direction. He wondered what was going on, but quickly concluded that there was some form of danger behind them, judging by the way they were running.

Without asking what the matter was, he joined the people running, as they scampered in different directions. When he got to a place of safety, he stopped to inquire what had triggered the sprint. This response he got was both infuriating and hilarious. The people said that they were not exactly sure, but they had heard a loud bang and suspected it was a gunshot. My friend had taken off running with this group of people, who weren't sure what they were running from either!

It is important to always get the facts before you join anything, even if it looks exciting and appealing. It is also equally important to be a leader and not a follower, because often times the follower does not ask questions, all they do is what they are instructed to do. Don't be like my friend, who ran a race that was unfruitful and wasn't his, to begin with.

Faith is not a fad.

Listen, faith is not a fad. It is not a get rich quick scheme or an easy way out of every challenge you face. On the contrary, faith is like a seed. You have to plant it in the right soil and constantly water it for it to grow. All this means is that you need to be consistent, persistent, and intentional.

Just because you are passionate and energetic, doesn't mean everything will easily fall into place, just because you show up. You have to believe in your success, visualize it, work towards it, and believe that God will be right there with you, making the impossible, become possible.

"Now faith is the substance of things hoped for, the evidence of things not seen." – **Hebrews 11:1**

Your faith is the only thing that can never be taken from you. The choice of what to believe is always yours. But remember, faith is not something you can fake. You can pretend to believe in something, but you cannot forge manifestation, and that's a fact.

Be inspired to be an explorer; a risk-taker. Explorers know that somewhere out there lies something that man has not put his hand on yet and they empower themselves to find it. There is something out there waiting for you to lay your hand on. Lift up your head and look to the horizon. Brace yourself and step out to reach out.

Listen, at some point in life you will have to take risks, and the only way to be an effective risk-taker is to have faith.

Christopher Columbus was a great explorer who sailed the seas and discovered America. He was prompted by thoughts of discovering the unknown worlds. His heart was telling him that there was more out there and that he should not settle only, for what he could see, right in front of him.

There is honor for those that will take the time to search out matters that develop human life and creation. Unfortunately, only a handful of people, take up the challenge to step out, to uncover these hidden gems. No wonder the world is ruled by a few powerful families, who have been enlightened in ways that are hidden from everyone else; they create and fully understand the systems of the world.

The point is, you cannot have greatness without faith, neither can you discover who you are without it. Everyone on earth has something they believe in and it is evident in what manifests in their lives. Your faith will always produce something, so if you want to see what you believe in, look at what has been manifesting in your life.

Begin to pay attention to what you believe in and if it does not align with your purpose or how you want your life to be, then you need to make some changes. I'll say it again, you only live once. Your faith will take you places you never even dreamt possible, because faith is always the gamechanger.

Faith by the day.

Do you remember when you were a kid and your parent or guardian grounded you, so you sat by the window and watched all the kids having a good time playing outside? That feeling of being trapped is what I felt one day.

It was an ordinary Sunday afternoon like every other. I had gone to church in the morning and was now headed home to pack a bag for my next trip. As I drove down the road in my late-model, Mercedes Benz, admiring the beautiful sunny day, I was suddenly overcome with the feeling of being trapped.

I began to wrestle with the feeling that there was something more; something I was missing out on. This feeling did not subside even as I drove to the airport. In fact, it got stronger and stronger, the farther I drove. I felt like a fraud, because I fit the bill of success on the outside in exchange for true happiness and fulfilment, at the core of my being.

This is the realization that slapped me in the face, in Ghana. My corporate card or my salary could not pay for faith by the day. What do I mean by this? I had faith for many things, but when I was confronted with the kind of faith that trusted God for provision **daily**, I fell short.

When I looked at the people living with this kind of faith versus the man I saw in the mirror, it broke my heart to realize that my faith was not strong. This was embarrassing and terrifying, but also upsetting.

"After all, I am a minister for God's sake," I thought to myself. "I have faith... Don't I?"

Have you ever had an awakening? My encounters in Africa were my continuous awakening, long after I had left and returned to the United States. This "awakening" had me question myself. There were times I'd be physically in meetings, but mentally and spiritually unavailable, because I'd be too busy arguing with myself and asking questions like, what the hell am I doing here? What percentage of my true talents and God-given abilities am I using?

Have you ever asked yourself these questions and been honest with yourself, about the answers? Or have you been convincing yourself for the longest time, that you are in the right place and you are maximizing your God-given talents.

The answer for me was 10%. Yes, when I truly evaluated my life and what I was doing, I was shocked to see that it was not even half of the capacity, God had deposited within me. So, if I wasn't even utilizing half of my true talents and abilities, why was I still in corporate America? The same reason you probably still are, and that is the fact that I lacked faith.

The difference between the people I met in Ghana and us here, is they operated with confidence and conviction in God, while we operate with confidence and conviction in our glass ceiling (our pay checks). We look at the comfort and stability that our pay checks afford us and put our trust in it, instead of the one who created everything; the one from whom all blessings flow.

I did not realize back then, that true faith in God destroys the glass ceiling. It breaks down mental and financial barriers, and makes your earning capability reach whatever height your faith can go. Now I know some people may scoff at this, and look at the people in Ghana as poor when in actual fact, they were richer than the majority of us, because they had everything they asked God for.

Think about it; we all have a definition of being wealthy. To them, being wealthy was having a warm meal, love, laughter, and peace. They were not interested in fancy gadgets, clothes, or a fat bank balance; all that mattered to them was, they had one another, and love enabled them to work hard and share everything they had.

Those hardworking people would sell windshield wipers, having never even owned a vehicle. Others would make all sorts of items out of raw materials, all to feed their families. And do you know what was even more amazing? They never complained, even if they only made one sale. They were happy, as long as their families were fed that day.

This experience challenged everything who I thought I was. I was materially rich but poor in faith! With this realization came the thought that I was not the only one. I began to wander far outside of myself and thought of how many other people lived this way; surely, I was not the only one.

Are you materially rich, but poor in faith? If every account you had hit ZERO today, what would you do? Would you call every financial institution you can think of, and beg for a loan? Or will you stay calm and believe that The Lord will provide? Will the faith you have right now, be able to sustain you and see you through?

CHAPTER 8

THE 90-YEAR-OLD YOU WOULD SAY, "GO FOR IT!"

In many of my travels I've met very different people; people of all ages, races and creeds, and I have to say, the most interesting people I've had the pleasure of speaking to have been the elderly. There's just something profound about their outlook on life that inspired and motivated me to live each day to the fullest.

If you've ever had a conversation with an elderly person, then you'll know how wholesome these conversations can be. When I asked each of them if they had any regrets in life, the common denominator in their answers were their jobs/careers. These wonderful people who had seen many moons wished they had followed their dreams, while they still had the energy in their bodies to do so.

See, the older you get, the more natural strength leaves your body. You find that at 60 you are unable to perform the same way you did when you were 25. Not that you are unable at that age, but your effectiveness is lower than when you were in your twenties, because nature takes its course; age slows us down.

Time is very precious, I'm sure you've heard it a thousand times, however, it remains true. You wouldn't want to look back on your life one day and wish you had lived differently. Seize the opportunities while you still can, chase your crazy dream while you still have the strength in your bones. Just do what makes you happy while you still have the energy to enjoy it, because once a moment is gone, it will never return.

"A man who dares to waste one hour of time has not discovered the value of life." ~ *Charles Darwin*

I read an article about a 94 year old gymnast and it blew me away! Johanna Quaas, hailing from Germany, is the oldest active gymnast, and she is still as strong and graceful as ever. As we all know, life happens, and it messes up our plans unexpectedly. This is what happened to Ms. Quaas. Somewhere along the line, she had to give up her dream, but at the age of 57, she was inspired to pick it up again and she is still going strong to this day.

The point of this story is that life happens. There will always be something that will get in the way of you following your passion. For some people it is a life-altering situation, and for others, life just gets busy or situations get out of their control, all happening at once and overwhelming them, but don't give up!

It is far better to look back on your life one day and be at peace with yourself, knowing that you fulfilled all you wanted to, chased that crazy dream, or started that business, rather than look back with regret, wishing you could turn back the hands of time.

For me, on paper, I had it all. In reality, something was missing. When I looked at my day to day life, I realized what I was doing, no longer fulfilled me. Feeling this way had nothing to do with my work environment, seniors, or hours. I wasn't dissatisfied with my job at all.

On the contrary, I thought I'd be in that position until retirement, when I could kick back, relax, and pat myself on the back, for doing a great job all those years. But you see, God showed me, through my encounters with other people, that the plans He had for my life were far greater and more fulfilling, than what I thought was the best for me.

Think of it this way: you're on your way to a festival and you are in your car driving at 25 mph, on the freeway. You're moving slower than everyone else, which frustrates you, but at the same time, you feel safe and in control of your vehicle, so you maintain your speed. Suddenly a police officer asks you to pull over and tells you that you need to drive faster, but you argue that if you drive faster you will have less control of the vehicle and get into an accident, because there are other vehicles around you. You then carry on at the same speed, but then you arrive at the festival 10 minutes before it ends, and everyone is already walking and talking about how great it was.

A lot of people are living their lives at 25 mph, thinking they will arrive at the destination anyway, but they don't take into account the experience they would be missing out on until it's too late. Don't be one of those people. Don't be the kind of person who misses out on the joys of life, because you are more focused on hitting all the "right" steps to success.

You might think your success lies in the corporate world, and you might be right, but if you've gotten this far in the book, then chances are you have that feeling in your bones, that there is something else out there for you that you are too afraid to reach out to.

It's Never Too Late!

"I'm too old."

"My time has passed."

"It's too late for me."

These are words I've heard many times before. It's as though people think that the more they age, the less valid their dreams become, but that simply isn't true. Who said there is an age limit on what you can achieve? Yes, it is better to do certain things when you are young, but that does not mean they cannot be done when you are old.

Age is more of a state of mind than a state of your physical body.

I love it when I see senior citizens doing activities that are not the norm for people their age. Activities such as Salsa dancing, scavenger hunts, Zumba on the beach or in a park, taking a class, and any other activity, they are normally ruled out of. These individuals are living testimonies that age isn't an excuse to not pursue your passion.

If you visit most major cities in the world, there is a little sense of peace and joy when you see the familiar bright yellow M. That's right, I'm talking about McDonald's. This global franchise was founded by a man named Ray Kroc, at the age of 52. These days, people in their 50's are already looking forward to retirement, but for Ray, that is when his dream came alive.

The grace of God enables us to go where we have never gone and to do what we have never done before, but you also have to take a step of faith. You might think you are past the age to achieve something, but the question is, have you even tried? While others use old age as an excuse, others use young age as the reason they are not successful or are not doing anything at all.

Have you noticed that more and more teenagers are becoming millionaires these days? Even in the corporate world, the workforce is becoming younger and younger, so there is no excuse whether young or old, because time and chance happen to all of us. Opportunities are presented to all of us, you just have to recognize them.

I have learned the correlation between valuing my time and succeeding at my goals. Get rid of excuses. If you keep looking for reasons as to why you cannot do something, trust me, you will find more than you imagined. So forget your age, race, gender, and shortcomings and just do it. It's as simple as that.

Change is possible for anyone who can see an opportunity, even in a negative circumstance and take a leap of faith to grab it. When you discover how to see the beauty in the midst of the storm, your eyes will be open to opportunity all around you, even in the least likely of places.

There is no such thing as a stupid idea!

There is no such thing as a stupid idea, except for the small minded people you're spending time with. Remember back in school when the teacher would group you with other students for a project and you had to brainstorm? I can guarantee that you heard the words, "That's dumb," at least one time in your life, regardless of whether or not it was directed to you. I know from experience, how discouraging it can be when your ideas are not well received by your peers, but letting someone's opinion dictate your decisions, is one of the biggest mistakes anyone can ever make in life.

It all boils down to perspective. To one person your idea might be stupid, but to another, it might be the solution to a problem they've been facing. Therefore, don't allow one person's opinion to become the compass that guides your life's journey. If your business idea or talent is not well received, look for another audience and try again.

Take carpenters for instance. They are critical thinkers who possess insight into trees most people don't have. Trees/wood translate into many things in their sight: tables, chairs, beds, cupboards, roof trusses, and other things that are functional and can generate income. The rest of us, on the other hand, see trees as a source of shade to relax under on a hot day, or we see them as part of an aesthetic. So you and a carpenter can look at the same tree, but see different functions. Does that mean one of you is wrong? Absolutely not.

Life is all about perspective. People might ridicule you for leaving your fancy job to start a restaurant, become an educator, or travel the world, because in their sight you are ruining your life, but ask yourself this question, "Who am I living for?"

Don't let your life be that way. Don't give other people the power to dictate what you do with your life. People will always have opinions, but their opinions are not facts. At the end of the day, you are responsible for your life and the choices you make. You don't want to look back one day and regret not having done what you wanted. Remember, some people are not comfortable seeing you in the success that you're destined for. Let me say it a different way. Shallow people are okay with you going nowhere, right along with them.

Don't put off your dreams for another day or for when you retire, because you will regret it. Life keeps moving forward regardless of whether or not we move forward with it. World changers are people who refuse to be prisoners of their own comfort. Nothing worthwhile comes easy, which is why you have to be resilient. Dreamers don't stop at anything until they see the fulfillment of their dream.

Don't settle for less.

I always refer to J.K. Rowling, the legendary author of the Harry Potter Series, because her story inspires me. Did you know that before her big break she was a broke, single mother who was living with depression while she took care of her kids, studying and writing her books, all at the same time? She is now one of the richest women in the world, living a beautiful and comfortable life, but her journey to get there was far from pretty. But everything she endured and overcame, made her the woman she is today; it made her the amazing author who has undoubtedly given the world one of the best bodies of literature.

"It's impossible to live without failing at something, unless you live so cautiously that you might as well not have lived at all- in which case, you fail by default."– *J.K. Rowling*

Rowling, from her former life description, was by no means a happy woman. She had everything working against her, but refused to settle for any less than what she knew she deserved. She persevered against all odds and now she is a living testimony that you can do great things, even if everything around you doesn't seem to align with your choices.

"Are you truly happy Mark?" I asked myself one day, and I couldn't answer that question. What had changed? You see, I was truly happy with my job; I enjoyed what I did. I felt good about my job and the fact that I could provide for my family. Everything was going just as I had planned it, which is not something everyone can confidently say about their lives, but it was true for me. But after my experience on my way back from Africa, I realized that I couldn't accurately answer that question.

I had just come from a place where people were ever joyous and they barely had anything as I mentioned before. Their lives were all about faith and nothing else. I wanted that. I wanted that true joy that radiated from deep within my soul.

Imagine if J.K. Rowling allowed the opinions of the people around her and the gravity of her situation, to deter her from writing? The world would have never known Harry Potter, which is something I believe she would have come to regret later on in life, had she not written it.

Set aside pride, excuses, fear, etc., and have faith that God will fulfill what He has begun in you. So what is holding you back from living a great life?

Your baggage from your past and present season should not be taken into your next season of life; carrying it over can be crippling to your dream. Imagine getting married and taking the memories of your previous romantic relationships into your marriage? The past is great for life experience, but it is not meant to be carried into your future.

If I asked you right now, "Are you happy in your life," what would your honest answer be? I'm not asking if you are excited about your life, because excitement has a lot to do with a particular moment or an achievement; it is a fleeting feeling. I'm asking about the aftermath of the celebration and emotional hype. I'm asking about your day to day life.

Many people are doing things for convenience's sake and not because they are happy. You don't have to be one of those people. You can be happy, truly happy when you find the place where you belong. In order to be the best version of yourself, you must discover your life's purpose and have the courage to pursue it.

I was happy serving in corporate America for over two decades. I have no regrets whatsoever. I enjoyed serving my company. I'm grateful and will cherish that part of my life with all the amazing people who were a part of my experience; they contributed greatly to who I am today and I wish them well. I know that you don't become great in life without the contribution of other people.

But that part of my life in corporate America expired. It no longer brought me excitement and happiness, as before and if I continued on that path, my life was going to be miserable. Miserable, not because there was something wrong at my workplace or with colleagues, but because I'd be living out of sync with my purpose and the time had come to get in line with it.

Living in alignment with your purpose is what brings true happiness. This is when you know that you know, that you know you're doing what you are supposed to be doing and it brings fulfillment in your life.

It also allowed me to be a blessing to other people who needed assistance and for me, it felt good to be a helping hand. The bible does say "It is more blessed to give than to receive," and I feel blessed and happy to contribute to someone's happiness. For this, I'll always be grateful to both God and my employers, for giving me such a life changing opportunity.

I'm grateful for the professional development I gained over those two decades of service with them. I was able to meet influential people and immerse myself in different cultures, as I traveled to different places in the world, and that is something about my career that I will cherish. I met extremely intelligent, diverse, and assertive individuals who were at the same time spontaneous, positive, and growth-oriented; traits I have now taken personal pride in upholding as well.

I must say that I'm grateful also to the individuals that were a thorn in my flesh, you know why? They helped to shape me into the man I am today; they were effective in pushing me to work harder, smarter, and sharpen my abilities, which ushered me to the top of the ladder. They provoked me to prove myself, aim higher, and stand out.

Everyone who crosses our path whether good or bad, plays an important role in our life, if we look closely that is. Our bad experiences expose us to what we could not discover during good times. It's a case of the rejected stone becoming the chief cornerstone- something that is important for the structural integrity of the building. How would we know what was good if there was nothing bad?

"All things works together for the good of those who love the Lord and are called to his purpose" - **Romans 8:28**

This scripture is a reminder to appreciate, what life throws at you, whether good or bad because they are all lessons that mold your character and encourage you to never settle. Don't wait for time to pass you by. Don't wait until you're old and frail to wish you could do what you're already wishing for now. Cast aside your doubt and fear and go for it!

CHAPTER 9

THE TIME WILL NEVER BE RIGHT

One of the biggest lessons I've learned in life is, the right time will never come. What do I mean by this? There's something you've wanted to do for so long, but you've been putting it off either, because of fear or because you have other responsibilities that take priority, and more often than not, you end up not doing that one thing you wanted to do all along, because life gets in the way.

You've probably heard the adage "Strike while the iron is hot" and know that it refers to seizing opportunities or favorable conditions, when they are presented, but in this chapter, it means to pursue the idea while you still have the confidence.

We often don't need people to discourage us from pursuing our goals and dreams, because we talk ourselves out of it the majority of the time. Don't believe me? Well, think of the last time you were alone and had a brilliant idea that you didn't manifest into reality; who talked you out of it? Chances are, the more you thought about it, the more you convinced yourself that it was a terrible idea. This happens to all of us.

Think back to when you lost your faith and confidence in yourself and imagine what your life would have looked like today, had you chosen differently back then. The purpose of this exercise isn't so you beat yourself down and begin or continue to live in regret, but rather to help you realize that it's not too late to make a different decision.

"It was my fear of failure that first kept me from attempting the master work. Now, I'm beginning what I could have started ten years ago. But I'm happy at least that I didn't wait twenty years."
– Paolo Coelho

Timing is everything. Think of it this way, you can catch the next train if you miss the first one, but you'll never know what the journey on the first train would have been like, nor the people you would have met. But most importantly, it will take you longer to arrive at your destination, meaning you would have wasted valuable time.

Almost every entrepreneur I've met has told me that they put off starting their business, because they thought the time was not right. Some thought the timing would be perfect when they had saved up enough money, while others thought the timing would be perfect when the economy picked up, and each one ended up wasting years waiting for the perfect time, which never came.

This is a lesson we all need to learn in life. The 'perfect time' does not exist. It is a fairytale idea that society has created to excuse procrastination. It is a term that absolves us, of the guilt of succumbing to fear, and putting off our goals and dreams for 'later.'

Remember, tomorrow is not promised. No one knows how much time they have on this earth, so don't put things off for another day, because that day might not come.

Confront your fears!

What is holding you back from following your dreams? We all have our own mountains to overcome. These fears seem to manifest when the season of transition comes. Haven't you noticed that when the time to move on to better things or promotion arrives, all kinds of problems begin to pop up from every direction? For example, if your colleagues learn that a promotion is available for someone in your department and you are the top candidate, you will begin to face animosity from some of them, or maybe even sabotage.

In all my years I've witnessed many people get promoted, but I've also heard a lot of excuses, which pose these questions: Why are we so afraid of change? What is it about change that terrifies us to the point of stagnation, or worse, retreat?

Why is it that negative thoughts plague our minds when we are faced with opportunities? And why do we entertain them? We have given fear too much power in our lives and become victims of things that don't even exist.

But you know, there's always that "What if" that cancels and overrides the negative thoughts. When I felt it was time to leave the corporate world, I encouraged myself by challenging my negative thoughts with, "What if this becomes one of the greatest things that has ever happened to me?" I knew I was not prepared to miss this opportunity to step into something better. Remember, that huge excitement, yet crazy scared at the same time!

I believe the best for my life had been kept until that very moment. I motivated myself until the fear left me. Because I had purposed to play my part before leaving this world, I confronted my fears and made up my mind to go after my dream. With time, the conviction that I was making the right choice got stronger and stronger.

"Waiting is a trap. There will always be reasons to wait – The truth is, there are only two things in life, reasons and results, and reasons simply don't count." – *Robert Anthony*

Stop looking back at all the time you've lost and make that choice to start today. The longer you put it off, the more time is wasted. You can pursue your destiny, as long as you have breath in your lungs.

Tomorrow may not be promised, but today is. Accept that you've made mistakes, but don't beat yourself up about it. Release yourself and move on. If you have to relocate, go ahead and move. If it's a relationship you need to mend, swallow your pride and go fix it. But, always remember that the time you waste not doing what you're meant to be doing, is time lost forever.

Life has seasons.

There are many seasons in life, and with each new season comes change. The opportunities you miss in one season may never repeat themselves again. This is why it is important that you seize every moment and every opportunity, to do what you need to do, in alignment with your purpose, goals, and dreams.

Many people are master procrastinators. If you are one of these people, then you probably live with a lot of regrets. But, wishing you could go back in time and change things, only causes stagnation in your present and blinds you to the possibilities that could be your future. So stop saying "I'll do it tomorrow," or "I'll do it later when I have the time," because the truth is that there will never be a right time.

You have to make time for what you value because no one else will.

"To everything there is a season, A time for every purpose under heaven: A time to be born, And a time to die; A time to plant, And a time to pluck what is planted;

A time to kill, And a time to heal; A time to break down, And a time to build up; A time to weep, And a time to laugh; A time to mourn, And a time to dance; A time to cast away stones, And a time to gather stones; A time to embrace, And a time to refrain from embracing;

A time to gain, And a time to lose; A time to keep, And a time to throw away; A time to tear, And a time to sew; A time to keep silence, And a time to speak; A time to love, And a time to hate; A time of war, And a time of peace." – Ecclesiastes 3:1-8 (NKJV)

Sometimes your dreams will require that you change your location. This is challenging, because you have to sacrifice your place of comfort and familiarity for the unknown. It is a heavy burden to bear, especially if you have a family. But you see, the size of your dream determines the level of your sacrifice, and relocation is one of the major reasons people put off their dreams. But new places mean new adventures, new beginnings, new opportunities, and sometimes it is just the kick we need, to fully commit to going after the desires of our hearts. Don't feel guilty for having to leave everything and everyone, in pursuit of your purpose. It may be sad and painful, but nothing compares to the feeling of living life feeling unfulfilled.

New seasons will challenge many areas of your life, especially relationships. People you love and have built memories with may even view this as selfishness or even try to guilt-trip you into changing your mind, but there comes a time in life where you have to put yourself first.

Statements I personally think are abused by society are, "You've changed" or "You're not who you used to be," or even worse, "You think you're better than us." These statements are not only disheartening, but they have also played a major role in hindering numerous people from pursuing their passion.

It seems like most of us are so afraid of hearing the words, "You've changed," because of the negative connotation associated with them. But here's the thing, change is good! Hearing those words mean you are making progress in life.

People don't want you to change; that's just a fact. Most people want you to remain at the same level or lower than they are. It makes them feel accomplished. So when they say "You've changed," they are trying to keep you stagnant, because it benefits their image.

Others will be challenged by your boldness and some will shun you for it, because they want to selfishly keep you in mediocrity along with themselves, or they want a squad (with you in it) to cheer them on as they chase their dreams. But you have to break out of this. Best believe that not everyone who claims to love you, or even like you, has your best interests at heart. This is why you should not stand back for anyone or try to fit your life into someone's timeline or idea of success. When the time for change comes, you had better jump up and grab it with both hands, because no one will ever do it for you.

New seasons may also introduce new variables. Plans may change with the introduction of new variables into the equation. Sometimes, due to unforeseen circumstances like accidents, death, loss of income, marital differences, and health issues etc., we begin to view life from a new lens. This often changes how we think, how we react to situations, what we like, and dislike, accept and tolerate.

This is all the more reason that you do not waste any more time. Take what each day has in store for you and do what it requires. None of us can afford to lose something as precious as time. If you keep waiting for the right time you might end up waiting forever.

Make room for growth.

Growth is a painful, yet necessary part of life. It is painful in the sense that you have to leave people and things behind, that don't align with your current season. You may find that you prefer staying in rather than going out, or you might end up just dropping every habit that is not beneficial to your new path.

When I look at my own life in the light of all these points I've mentioned so far, I can say that I have changed and grown in ways I never thought possible. I thought I had lived a full life and achieved everything there was to achieve, but God showed me that there was still a lot of room left for growth in me.

We tend to limit ourselves to achievements we think will bring us fulfillment and thus shut the doors of opportunities, ourselves. I've had colleagues whose sole ambition was to get a job in our company. After they got in, that fire sizzled out and they accepted that they had reached the peak of their achievements in life. Some of my counterparts in my field, weren't interested in promotions or new job opportunities, because they didn't want to "mess with the formula" of what worked. But there is no growth or opportunities in that mindset.

Today, I challenge you to write down all the changes/growth that you've gone through in the past year. This exercise will show you just how rapidly you're changing. Life continually requires us to change; to adapt. Technology has evolved. Society has evolved. The economy has evolved. Have you evolved?

"If we don't change, we don't grow. If we don't grow, we aren't really living." — *Gail Sheehy*

People don't pay much attention to what you say, but rather if you live out what you say. If they see a contradiction between the two, then they don't take you seriously, but if they see alignment between the two then they respect you. They'll take you at your word.

Accept the fact that things change and people change, because we are all in different seasons of life. Everybody's changing, so why do you want to remain the same? It's like buying a ticket for a connecting flight, but refusing to board a different plane when the time comes to make the change, and yet still expecting to arrive at your desired destination.

When my season to leave my job approached, I began to find flaws in my work environment and superiors, that I hadn't seen before. Not that they were flawed per se, but I had begun to evolve, therefore, I began to view things differently. All of a sudden, tasks I enjoyed doing began to frustrate me. The long hours I enjoyed working began to make me bitter for not having enough free time. Basically, I suddenly had issues with things that had never bothered me before.

I knew that my time in the corporate world had come to an end, but instead of walking away, I projected my frustrations on those around me.

Nothing around me changed except for me, which meant I no longer belonged in that space. Does this sound familiar?

The dissatisfaction and frustration that develops is a sign that you are about to enter into a new season. A longing for something different or new or feeling like something is missing in your life, is the sign you have been seeking. Your work no longer excites you; you dread Sundays because they lead to Mondays and you dread Mondays because they mean you have to work for at least five days. Somehow everything you once loved slowly begins to irritate you. All of this means it is time for a change.

The season of my career in corporate America spanned over two decades before it expired. Yours may be less or more than mine. Whatever the case may be, when the time comes for your season to change, will you be ready? Or will you try to hold onto the very thing that makes you miserable and sick?

One may ask, "Well, when is it the right time to change?" Again, this is personal and it has nothing to do with age, gender, or your background, but has everything to do with what the creator predestined for each one of us. Remember this, "one man's meat may be another man's poison." Make sure you're walking in your season and not someone else's. Stop waiting for the perfect time. Instead, embrace growth and allow yourself to evolve with your environment.

Every minute is the perfect time to start. You don't have to wait for opportunities; you can create them.

Here's a story, an analogy, for you to consider:

Most all of us have seen, read or heard about the wonderful Wizard of Oz. We all know that little Dorothy was in search of finding a way back home. Once she heard about this "Wizard" who could make it happen, her next step and primary goal, was figuring out how she could get to the Wizard of Oz.

We know she was told to "follow the yellow brick road" and once she did, she met the Lion, the Tin Man, and the Scarecrow. What's the point here?

You, just like Dorothy, have all of the resources that you need to get to the Wizard. You simply have to START WALKING and what you need will come along your journey down the yellow brick road!

CHAPTER 10

IT'S WORTH THE BATTLE

The journey will not be easy. That's just a fact. If you think it will be smooth sailing because you've chosen to do what you love, then think again. This path will probably be more difficult than getting into the corporate world, but rest assured, it is worth the battle.

When you think of battle, the mind immediately pictures large, impressive armies with heavy artillery, looking menacing, but very rarely would one say they thought about the battle strategy.

The battle will absolutely be worth it, when you can look back on it one day and celebrate your victory, but the reality is, there are some steps that should be followed before the battle. I can assure you that leaving the corporate world to pursue your passions is one of the most fulfilling accomplishments you will ever have in life. However, the day will come when you will feel like quitting. It happens to all of us.

The most successful people in the world today are people who had numerous opportunities to quit and didn't. I always reference Steve Jobs, because there are a lot of lessons that can be learned from his life.

The fact alone, that he was fired from a company he co-founded, to this day, is mind-blowing! That dream that you have right now; what if you amass great success, only to be removed from the very thing you created? How would you feel? But more importantly, would you recover from that?

Remarkably, Steve Jobs carried on as though nothing had happened. Of course, we don't know how he was dealing with it behind closed doors, and that is the point. He was hit with arguably the biggest curveball, but not once did he allow anyone to see him crumble. He was so confident in his vision that he didn't quit, even when quitting would have been acceptable. That set a standard for me, and hopefully for you too. In the end, Mr. Jobs' continued pursuit paid off. In other words, it was all worth it in the end. But you see, everyone wants the fluffy rainbows and sunshine, version of success when in reality, it is a difficult journey.

Personally, I have over 20 years of experience in my field, but being an author, missionary, and entrepreneur, hold different challenges than my job in corporate. I'm learning new things every day and constantly fighting battles I never even knew existed, and honestly, quitting has crossed my mind. But that's all I allowed it to do... cross my mind. I have a WINNER'S MENTALITY! Quitting has never, and will never, be an option! And by the way, I DO NOT have a plan B!

That's my FAITH coupled with my WORKS! How about you? It's a winner's mentality that will fuel you to press on no matter what comes in your way. I promise you, it really is worth it in the end, so don't entertain thoughts and opinions that will bring you down. Instead, focus on preparing for the exciting journey you are about to take. I mean, have you ever gone on a trip without doing research on your destination or packing a suitcase? Even when you take "spontaneous" trips, there's a small level of research or planning that goes into it, because technology has made it so easy.

Plan your Departure.

Following your dreams is exciting. Just the thought may make you want to get up and go right this instant. Slow down! Take a breath, and take a seat. You need to plan first.

Imagine going to the bank in need of a loan, to launch your business, and telling the banker, you don't have a business plan, you just have a dream. It sounds foolish, doesn't it? DO you think any bank or lending institution would lend you even a dime? No!

Just because you have an amazing dream and the desire to quit corporate America, does not mean you should dive in headfirst without direction. You don't see skydivers jumping out of planes without parachutes, just as you don't see entrepreneurs asking for crowdfunding without a business proposal. By not having a plan, you will directly kill the very dream you are trying to bring to life.

One of the biggest mistakes most new entrepreneurs make is not planning adequately, or at all. Now, it might seem counter-intuitive to take time to plan for your next step, because that requires staying right where you are a little longer, but it is necessary, and it could be the difference between success and failure, in your future ventures.

When I felt the desire to quit, I didn't walk into my boss' office with a resignation letter in hand the very moment I arrived back in the US. Instead, I took the time to plan, pray, and prepare. If I had allowed my excitement to rule me, I probably would have gone back and begged for my job a month, weeks, or even days after quitting.

Just because you have a big dream does not mean you should be reckless. Most of us tend to make the mistake of wanting to leave things up to chance, when in reality, the majority of success was as a result of planning. Of course, you can't plan for everything, neither can you predict or guarantee your success, but planning will provide a clearer picture to help you navigate your way in the entrepreneurial world. Bear in mind, becoming your own boss means all the responsibility rests on your shoulders 24/7, which means you will have to make some major sacrifices along the way. This is why planning is so important. The plan doesn't have to be extensive, but you should at least have one.

"Always plan ahead. It wasn't raining when Noah built the ark." — *Richard Cushing*

Here's an interesting real-life story of a man who didn't know the importance of preparation:

A man took his nephew to a local swimming pool for a swim. Upon arrival, he took his nephew to the kiddies pool, where there was supervision, and proceeded to the adult pool. Now, the issue here was that the man had never been to a swimming pool prior to that day, neither had he received swimming lessons or instructions in a body of water.

The man stood to the side at first, observing the various activities people were engaging in, when his eyes landed on a kid on the diving board. The kid looked confident and comfortable and seemed to only be a few years older than the man's nephew. With this in mind, the man decided to try it out as well. He concluded that he could do it, because a kid was doing it. So he climbed up the ladder, walked to the edge of the diving board, and dove straight into the deep end of the pool.

What followed next was a series of blood-curdling screams as his head bobbed in and out of the water. He didn't know how to swim!

Fortunately, the lifeguards came to his rescue, but as soon as he was taken out of the pool, he hightailed it out of there and vowed never to return.

As hilarious as this story may be, the truth is that most of us approach life this way; with little to no preparation. This is what often results in failure. Instead, ask questions. Gather as much information as you can, and don't be afraid to admit that you need help. Throw all pride aside and recognize every opportunity to learn something new.

"Our goals can only be reached through a vehicle of a plan, in which we must fervently believe, and upon which we must vigorously act. There is no other route to success." — *Pablo Picasso*

Don't look back.

Do not be afraid to try, even if you fail a few times. I never imagined I'd be a person who appreciates failure as much as I do today. Failing means you actually tried. It means you had the courage to pursue your dream. But what failure also brings, are great life lessons as mentioned before. It is vital though, that you don't look back.

It can be tempting to look back at your comfort zone once you've jumped off the edge, but keep your eyes on the prize. Maintaining your focus will help you navigate through failure to find the lessons within it. What's even better is that failure gives you the opportunity to try a different, and possibly more effective, strategy.

"Never look back unless you are planning to go that way." – *Henry David Thoreau*

Stay focused and consistent. Yes, you have to do both. Julia Child released her first book at the age of 50, after spending the majority of her life unhappy in the advertising industry. This book has propelled Julia into becoming a celebrity chef. Similarly, Samuel L. Jackson was also older when he got his big break. He was 45 years old when he starred in the hit movie *Pulp Fiction*. Mr. Jackson's popularity only grew from that point, until he became a big Hollywood star.

You see, great breakthroughs come to people who remain consistent and refuse to quit; people who are willing to get down and dirty; people who are eager to experience new territories; people who are ready to stand out in the crowd. That's how great names are built. Great names are not for the spectators, but the players.

Choose to be a player, not a spectator.

You will be faced with opposition whether you like it or not. There is no success without forces working against your pursuits. It's in these circumstances your hunger is tested. If your hunger for success is lacking, then you will settle for a bowl of soup; but if your hunger is stronger, no power can stop you from getting to the top.

Keep pushing on!

Determined people see the end from the beginning. They seal the deal before the bidding starts. They make up their minds not to settle for anything but their expectations and also, not to let anyone take their glory. They go after their dream with all they have.

Don't waste your life as a spectator. It doesn't pay. Get involved. Put on your jersey and your boots and step onto the field with the determination to win. I know how terrifying it is to step into the unknown, but I can assure you, it is worth it, but you have to stay committed. Stay in the game and stay committed until the final whistle is blown.

"Have I not commanded you? Be strong and of good courage; do not be afraid, nor be dismayed, for the Lord your God is with you wherever you go." – Joshua 1:9

I was told a story in Africa, of a young couple taking an evening stroll in a bushy and isolated area; promising to stay faithful to each other no matter what came their way. The man, assuring his partner emphatically, that he would stand by her side till death do them part. He had hardly completed this sentence when they heard the earth-shaking roar of a lion, coming from the nearby bush. Guess what? The guy took off running for his life, leaving the woman behind. She followed behind him crying and screaming, "You promised that you will stick with me no matter what!" But the guy just kept going without looking back, because his dear life was at stake. He yelled back to her that he didn't include a lion in the promise.

I saw myself in this story. I realized that I could talk a big game, but my words were not followed by commitment (action). I finally found my purpose, but I spent more time talking about it than I did acting upon it.

Have you ever hyped yourself up so much about doing something, but when the time came to do it you backed out? We've all been there and we've all done that. I had a crystal clear picture of what I wanted to achieve, but I was too afraid to press on towards my goal. Like the young man in the story above, I talked about greatness, but I had conditions.

Here's a challenge: Ask five people in your life what their passion is, and if they are not doing that particular thing, ask them why not.

I talk to young people about their goals and dreams all the time and the most common feedback I get from them are conditions in which they will pursue their dream. For example, an incredibly talented young woman was hiding the fact that she could sing. When she was caught singing to herself, in the mirror and asked why she wasn't pursuing a career in music, her response was that she wanted to be a singer, but she didn't want people to hear her sing. Imagine that!

Upon questioning her further, she revealed the ideal conditions in which she would release her gift, and these conditions included private recording sessions with only one producer in the studio, and not booking any shows with large audiences. She said that she preferred to remain hidden and just do her own thing privately. Like this young woman, you may have this big dream that you hope to achieve one day, but you have set too many unrealistic conditions that have become more of a hindrance than a preference.

Listen, you have to push forward whether the conditions are favorable or not. Be smart and be proactive, but don't be unreasonable. Life does not play by anyone's rules but God. So don't wait to feel comfortable enough to make your move. Plan for it, and then go for it.

Keep pushing on regardless of the perils of life that you will inevitably face. After all, no one said this would be easy, remember?

Remember the physician I met at the airport who quit his job? He may not have had a solid plan in place at the time, but I can assure you he had enough finances to back him until he came up with one. But even so, he had to have come up with a plan at some point in time.

The point is, don't stop. Don't give up along the way because you don't have it all figured out or because things are not going the way you imagined. Keep pushing on no matter how difficult your journey becomes, because that will make your victories that much greater.

You've got this! You are capable of so much more than you think. You are stronger than you give yourself credit for. Don't settle for anything less than greatness!

CONCLUSION

Your palms may be sweating and your knees trembling, but I tell you, nothing will compare to the feeling of taking charge of your life. It is both exciting and terrifying, but at the end of the day, it will be the most at peace your heart has ever been.

Greatness is waiting for you to take up the charge. There are few things in life I am absolutely certain of, and one of them is that you will never look back on your life with regret, once you get on your path to purpose.

If there is anything the COVID-19 pandemic has taught us, it is that the time to be fruitful is now. There is no better time than the present. As terrible as the pandemic has been, it has also been an instrument in bringing out people's talents, passions, and creativity. It's amazing how a 16-year-old following their passion became the one providing for their family when the pandemic struck, or how housewives who thought they weren't good at anything, have created flourishing businesses.

No matter how many times a road is traveled, no journey looks the same, but the destination never changes. Everyone is alive for a purpose, but not everyone is living their purpose. Why are you alive? What brought you to this book? That thing; that burning passion within your bones is what you should be pursuing, and I believe you will make the right choice.

Nobody wants to burn the boat and swim. Neither does anyone want to abandon the boat. The boat is safer, more comfortable, and requires less responsibility and courage. But the issue with being on the boat is that you are heading towards a predetermined destination. Someone else has already decided the direction and you are there to row that boat (labor) for that person. What happens when you've labored and run out of strength, though?

Life is finite. I cannot stress that enough. The majority of us take time/life for granted. Yet it is the most precious thing anybody can possess. The legacy you create is what remains when you pass on. That office or cubicle you claim as yours will be given to someone else when you are replaced. By spending your life laboring for someone else, you are merely writing the pages of their legacy. But what about you? It is time for you to live! It is time for you to take back control of your finances, time, and decisions. It is time for you to be who God created you to be.

No more excuses. No more delays. The time will never be right, so just go for it. Anything you want to achieve is possible if you back it up by FAITH!

I bargained with Life for a penny,
And Life would pay no more,
However I begged at evening
When I counted my scanty store;
For Life is just an employer,
He gives you what you ask,
But once you have set the wages,
Why, you must bear the task.
I worked for a menial's hire,
Only to learn, dismayed,
That any wage I had asked of Life,
Life would have paid.

- Jessie B. Rittenhouse

What are you asking life for?
I dare you to ask for more!
Burn the boat!
There is much more in store!
Faith and trust
Oh yes, that's a must!
Follow your dreams
Take them off the shelf
No matter how hard it seems
Be true to yourself!
Burn the boat!

Blessings to you on your new journey!

Sincerely,

Mark A. Davis

More Books Coming Soon!

The "Double My Income" Formula

Switch!

MARK A. DAVIS

Made in the USA
Columbia, SC
19 March 2021